The Growth of Mind

The Growth of Mind is the product of a series of ten lectures by Neville Symington. It offers an understanding of the mind and its capacity to discover truth, establishing this as the foundation stone for our judgement and critique of the human world. Although the book's field of exploration lies in psychological processes met in the consulting-room, grounded in the general principles of psycho-analysis, the book's mode of enquiry is to elucidate a knowledge of individual people.

Exploring the mind's *active* role in understanding, the book suggests that the act of understanding has a transformative function, and that to be a person is to be a part of a community. It suggests that the super-ego is a sign of some undeveloped function within the personality. If the ego and all its functions are fully evolved, then the super-ego will only be minimally present in the personality. Symington posits that the unconscious represents an agglomerative mass in an undifferentiated and indistinguishable state, rather than a realm of distinguishable thoughts or feelings that are not currently present to consciousness. The book attempts to understand better what this unconscious state is like and how we can think about it, underpinned by the belief that the better we understand it, the more its structure changes.

The Growth of Mind is aimed at professionals and researchers who have a basic understanding of the mind and its mode of operating. It will help readers become aware of this knowledge, strengthening it in the process and allowing it to become a foundational source of inspiration.

Neville Symington is a psycho-analyst in private practice in Sydney, Australia. As a young man he took a diploma in Philosophy and then in Theology. He later did a degree in Psychology and took a diploma in Clinical Psychology. He did his psycho-analytic training in London and is a Fellow of the British Psycho-Analytical Society. He held a senior staff position in the Adult Department of the Tavistock Clinic from 1977–85. He was also Chairman of the Psychology Discipline for the Adult and Adolescent Departments at the Tavistock Clinic in London. In 1986 he migrated to Sydney, Australia where he was Chairman of the Sydney Institute for Psycho-Analysis from 1987–93. He was President of the Australian Psycho-Analytic Society from 1999–2002. He is the author of *The*

Analytic Experience published by Free Association Press and St. Martins Press, of *Emotion and Spirit* published by Cassell and later re-published by Karnac Books, of *Narcissism: A New Theory*, *The Making of a Psychotherapist*, *The Spirit of Sanity*, *A Pattern of Madness*, *How to Choose a Psychotherapist*, *The Blind Man Sees*, *A Healing Conversation*, *Becoming a Person through Psycho-Analysis*, *The Psychology of the Person* and *A Different Path* which are all published by Karnac Books. He is joint-author with Joan Symington of *The Clinical Thinking of Wilfred Bion* published by Routledge. He also published a novel called *A Priest's Affair* published by Free Association Press and a book of poetry *In-gratitude and other Poems* published by Karnac.

In 2007 he started a clinical organization called Psychotherapy with Psychotic Patients (PPP). It had its first conference in February 2010 with Michael Robbins as keynote speaker together with himself and Jim Telfer. Its second conference with Carine Minne as guest analyst was in October 2016. He has lectured in Britain, Norway, Denmark, Poland, Portugal, Germany, Italy, the United States, Brazil, Israel, India, Japan, New Zealand and Australia. His website is: www.nevillesymington.com.

The Growth of Mind

Neville Symington

LONDON AND NEW YORK

First published 2019
by Routledge
2 Park Square, Milton Park, Abingdon, Oxon OX14 4RN

and by Routledge
711 Third Avenue, New York, NY 10017

Routledge is an imprint of the Taylor & Francis Group, an informa business

© 2019 Neville Symington

The right of Neville Symington to be identified as author of this work has been asserted by him in accordance with sections 77 and 78 of the Copyright, Designs and Patents Act 1988.

All rights reserved. No part of this book may be reprinted or reproduced or utilised in any form or by any electronic, mechanical, or other means, now known or hereafter invented, including photocopying and recording, or in any information storage or retrieval system, without permission in writing from the publishers.

Trademark notice: Product or corporate names may be trademarks or registered trademarks, and are used only for identification and explanation without intent to infringe.

British Library Cataloguing-in-Publication Data
A catalogue record for this book is available from the British Library

Library of Congress Cataloging-in-Publication Data
Names: Symington, Neville, author.
Title: The growth of mind / Neville Symington.
Description: Abingdon, Oxon ; New York, NY : Routledge, 2018.
Identifiers: LCCN 2018024945 (print) | LCCN 2018026716
 (ebook) | ISBN 9780429449079 (Master eBook) | ISBN
 9781138327818 (hardback) | ISBN 9781138327832 (pbk.)
Subjects: LCSH: Psychoanalysis. | Psychology.
Classification: LCC BF173 (ebook) | LCC BF173 .S8863 2018
 (print) | DDC 616.89—dc23
LC record available at https://lccn.loc.gov/2018024945

ISBN: 978-1-138-32781-8 (hbk)
ISBN: 978-1-138-32783-2 (pbk)
ISBN: 978-0-429-44907-9 (ebk)

Typeset in Times New Roman
by Apex CoVantage, LLC

Printed and bound in Great Britain by
TJ International Ltd, Padstow, Cornwall

Contents

	Introduction: on overview	1
1	The core of the personality	14
2	The unformed ego	31
3	Foundation for growth of mind	43
4	Consequences of mother's contemplation	51
5	Hypnotic power	62
6	Unfocussed stare	72
7	The knowledge of being	84
8	Creative intercourse between analyst and patient, between mother and child, between teacher and student	96
9	What is it that is unconscious?	107
	Index	114

Introduction
On overview

The goal of this book is to come to an understanding of the mind in general and its capacity to discover the truth and to establish this as the foundation stone for our judgement and critique of the human world. So this book is aimed at those who already understand the mind and its mode of operating. What is the purpose of imparting knowledge to someone who is already in possession of it? There are two reasons. One: that the person becomes a aware of the knowledge that he or she has and two: that hearing someone giving expression to what he or she knows strengthens this knowledge and thus it becomes an inspirational influence upon the many tributaries that derive from this knowledge lying at the root of the mind.

I will give you a personal example. Many years ago I studied Psychology at a university in England and I was taught learning theory à la Skinner, learnt that human learning was built on the same principles by which a rat learnt to run down one pathway in a maze and not another. Yet the greatest insights I have had within psychology came from an entirely different source; such as Giambattista Vico's theory of knowledge, or Soloviev's theory of personal morality and yet I did not believe what I had learnt. I was still too much in awe of those lecturers who had instilled into me the notion that human learning was the same as learning in animals. Then recently I read a book written by a compelling philosopher and psychiatrist who showed in the clearest light that it was precisely people like Vico or Soloviev who were truly psychologists and that those like Skinner and his comrades traded in a false coinage. I had known this but it took this new-found mentor to bring me to believe what I knew.

My field of exploration lies in the psychological processes that we meet in the consulting-room. The mode of enquiry is quite different to what I was taught when I started training at the Institute of Psycho-Analysis in London 45 years ago. I had been taught that there is a process going on in the patient which the analyst then needs to interpret and the interpretation of what is occurring brings what was hidden into consciousness. The analyst as a kind of spectator puts into words what he observes and the 'putting into words' makes what was unconscious conscious. For 'putting into words' the analyst relies on a model of the mind that he has learnt in his psycho-analytic schooling. Within psycho-analysis there are several different schools that find their embodiment in a corporate group of people. In London at the time when I trained there were three main schools: the classical Freudian, the Kleinian and the Independents. Each of these schools had key figures that actualized the thinking of the school over which they presided. So Anna Freud represented the classical Freudian school, Melanie Klein the Kleinian group and Winnicott and Balint the Independents. The clinical outlook was influenced, almost entirely, by the theoretical school of thinking into which the individual analyst had been inducted. There was then in this procedure a gathering of the individual into the belief system of the group. All these schools which have been mentioned and some which have not been mentioned are under the umbrella of psycho-analysis. Psycho-analysis itself has a definite creed. All human beings hide from themselves base motives that govern their behaviour. Every psychological act is composed of multiple motives. We tend to hide those motives which are base, self-diminishing or less praiseworthy. This is the position that psycho-analysis endorses. When Freud initiated this way of thinking he proposed a method by which the physician was able to elucidate this with a patient. Many of the tenets that are annunciated within psycho-analysis are general principles. What this book is concerned to elucidate is a knowledge not of general principles but of each individual person. No two people look exactly the same; no two people's minds are exactly the same. Psycho-analysis is crammed with theories, with generalizations, and, as the Greek philosopher, Stilpo, said, "Those who speak of men in general; speak of nobody".[1]

What this generalized perspective that I had been taught in my training missed out entirely was that a creation was occurring of what had not been present before. I can introduce this by quoting to you a personal experience. In 1979 I was reading a series of essays by Isaiah Berlin that were published in his book *Against the Current*.[2] The focus in the essays in this book is upon those European thinkers who went against the Enlightenment which was in high tide in the eighteenth century with Voltaire as its senior prophet. One such thinker whom he discusses is Giambattista Vico, born in 1668 and died in 1744. He was a philologist who taught in the University of Naples. Vico had started by being a faithful disciple of Descartes who taught that we know best the natural world which is just there and not created by human beings. Descartes thought that we know this better than the artefacts produced by human beings. This was the central belief governing the thinking of the Enlightenment: that we see things as they are which implies that our minds are robotic tape recorders; that our minds are governed by the inner and outer sensations that bombard the mind; that the mind is a lifeless slave to whatever impacts upon it. This was the view of John Locke whose belief that the mind is a *tabula rasa* governed thinking for the next two hundred and fifty years. But Vico underwent a somersault and strongly repudiated Descartes and the whole Enlightenment belief that it is only the natural world and its principles that can be faithfully known whereas man's own productions cannot be known with the same certainty as our knowledge of the natural world. We do not know what brought about this inner upheaval in Vico but, whatever it was, that produced this revolution in him, led him to proclaim 'No, Descartes is wrong – we know best what we have ourselves created.' This was absolutely mind-blowing when I read it in 1979. First: what I read had complete conviction for me. It seemed a simple statement but one that was so obvious that to refute it seemed absurd. If a painter and a photographer sat down in front of a lake surrounded by trees with some sheep and cows in a field to the left of the lake and the photographer clicked his machine and the painter drew colours from his palette to create the reflection of the trees with the differing light and this process took him five hours I felt sure that the painter knew that piece of landscape better than the photographer. I was, at the time of reading this book of Isaiah Berlin's, staying on the coast near Port Phillip Bay south of Melbourne in Australia and, per chance spending some time painting different sea-scapes and I knew that what I was seeing when I was creating through painting much better than when, on a previous occasion, I had clicked the camera. This statement of Vico's was a mental cataclysm. My mind would never be the same again. So, shortly after this earthquake of the mind, the thought came to me very quickly that if I can only truly know that which I have created then if the aim of psycho-analysis is to know myself which I believe is its essence then to achieve self-knowledge I had to create myself. This is a strange saying. There were events in my life that were lying there as dead corpses inside my soul and I needed to create them if I were truly to know them and thus know myself. Only by creating myself could I know myself. I will try to illustrate this strange statement shortly. Later this insight illuminated Bion's formulation of *alpha function* which I understood was this creative factor which Vico had taught me in so arresting a fashion. So I give this narrative in order to illustrate the difference between a generalized theory as opposed to an experience that was not general but singular, entirely personal and created.

Another aspect of this is that it is art not science that delineates the inner activities of human beings. Science examines the inanimate world, the non-human world and the unchangeable constants in the structure of human bodies. What Science studies in the human world is the particular form embodied in this mammal; in what ways it is similar to other mammals and the ways in which it is different. It examines for this purpose the structure and the behavioural activity of the human animal. Art however examines the way communication occurs within the human species and also penetrates and creates what humans do both within themselves and in relation to others.

Every system of thinking is underpinned by a belief and beliefs are always selective; because in a belief there is a particular focus which means other foci are either annihilated or diminished in their importance or significance. So, for example, Locke's view that the mind is a *tabula rasa* and all its knowledge is acquired through the ingestion of sensations which are turned into perceptions gives strength to one quality of mind but it ignores the mind as an active force, what Aquinas referred to as the *actus intellectualis*, that grasps reality itself. John

Henry Newman emphasized the way the mind grows through this formative power that it has:

> *The enlargement consists, not merely in the passive reception into the mind of a number of ideas hitherto unknown to it, but in the mind's energetic and simultaneous action upon and towards and among those new ideas, which are rushing upon it. It is the action of a formative power, reducing to order and meaning the matter of our acquirements; it is making the objects of our knowledge subjectively our own, or, to use a familiar word, it is a digestion of what we receive, into the substance of our previous state of thought; and without this no enlargement is said to follow.*[3]

The crucial sentence here is where he speaks of *a formative power, reducing to order and meaning the matter of our acquirements*. This *formative power* is another language for Bion's *alpha function* and what Newman refers to as the *matter of our acquirements* Bion refers to as *beta elements*. This essay of Newman which is a transcript of his lecture *Knowledge Viewed in Relation to Learning* which he gave in Dublin University in 1852 was a direct challenge to the pathway to knowledge that had been promoted by Locke and which has been followed by all but a few thinkers within the Social Sciences. Newman repudiated with powerful language the way Locke had formulated the mind's acquisition of knowledge. He was doing this because Locke's way of conceptualizing the activity of the mind was dominating in a strong way the scientific thinking in the nineteenth century.

Freud had a belief which underpinned some of his clinical suppositions. I quote one particular belief of his:

> *We . . . turn to the . . . question of what men themselves show by their behaviour to be the purpose and intention of their lives. What do they demand of life and wish to achieve in it? The answer to this can hardly be in doubt. They strive after happiness; they want to become happy and to remain so. The endeavour has two sides, a positive and negative aim. It aims, on the one hand, at an absence of pain and unpleasure, and, on the other, at the experiencing of strong feelings of pleasure.*[4]

But this belief has a selective focus as it obscures a different belief best expressed by the philosopher, John Macmurray:

> *Freedom is, I am assured, the pearl of great price for which, if we are wise, we shall be prepared to sell all our possessions, to buy it. The ancient and widespread belief that the supreme good of human life is happiness – for all its persuasiveness – is false. Freedom has a higher value than happiness; and this is what we recognize when we honour those who have been ready to sacrifice happiness, and even life itself, for freedom's sake.*[5]

So the mind needs to be open to both the belief systems articulated by Locke and by Newman and again that espoused by Freud and its opposite that was championed by Macmurray. Therefore the way we relate to any of these belief systems affects our behaviour towards other human beings, towards the lower animal world and also inanimate nature. If we take the position that one such system is the ultimate and all others false then this biases our way of connecting to another human being. We make him or her too consistent. Any devoted attachment to one belief means we falsify the complexity of human nature. Isaiah Berlin gives potent expression to this:

> *Systems are mere prisons of the spirit, and they lead not only to distortion in the sphere of knowledge, but to the erection of monstrous bureaucratic machines, built in accordance with the rules that ignore the teeming variety of the world, the untidy and asymmetrical inner lives of men, and crush them into conformity for the sake of some ideological chimera unrelated to the union of spirit and flesh that constitutes the real world.*[6]

Isaiah Berlin speaks of *prisons of the spirit* and it was a shock to me when I realized that any psycho-analytic doctrine was a *prison of the spirit* if it were applied without qualification when I was trying to understand a particular individual person. A crucial distinction needs to be made between that which is applicable to any human being and what is particular to this person here that I am in conversation with. A sculptor will fashion a head with a forehead, two eyes, two ears, a nose, two cheeks, a mouth and a chin. Looking at what he has produced will tell us that this is a human being and not a monkey or an elephant. But the particular form of this person's anatomy will differentiate him or her from any other person on the planet. So also we can apply this thinking to the mind. There are certain qualities of mind that are characteristic of all people but there are particular aspects and structures that are peculiar to John Smith alone or to Mary Jones alone. The analogy between the physical head of someone and the mind is not quite right because the difference of mind between one person and another is more fundamental as if, relying on the analogy, one had two eyes and another had only one. Certain mental abilities are almost absent in one person but hugely present in another. One man had a strong intuition of how his friend might be feeling but another had no sense of this at all. One had a vivid imagination, another was totally devoid of imagination. The place of imagination has been seriously underestimated in psycho-analytic discourse. I like this statement made by Mcneile Dixon:

> *If I were asked what has been the most powerful force in the making of history, you would probably adjudge me of unbalanced mind if I were to answer, as I should have to answer, metaphor, figurative expression. It is by imagination that men have lived; imagination rules all our lives. The human mind is not, as philosophers would have you think, a debating hall, but a picture gallery. Around it hang our similes, our concepts. The tyranny of the concept,*

as, for example, that modern one, which pictures the universe a machine . . . this tyranny of the concept is one from which the human mind never escapes. It hugs its self-imposed chains. . . . The prophets, the poets, the leaders of men are all of them masters of imagery, and by imagery they capture the human soul.[7]

* * *

There is early learning, almost an osmosis, which is often lacking in some particular area within the personality. A simple example: a man did not thank his wife when she brought him a gift from overseas and she was upset. This was not envy on his part; it was because he had not learnt how to thank. We tend to think that interactions like these are instinctive, that they do not have to be learnt but, on the contrary, the achievement of many such interpersonal activities are the product of early learning and this is not achieved by everyone. We even learn to see. People who are born blind and then in adulthood have an operation that enables them to see cannot initially see; they have to touch and feel an object first and only then are they able to see it. Richard Gregory in his excellent book *Eye and Brain* tells of a man aged 52 who had been blind from the age of ten months. He then had an operation where a donated cornea was implanted and then there was in him the ability to see but to be able to see an object he first needed to touch it. Gregory writes thus:

When he was just out of hospital, and his depression was but occasional, he would sometimes prefer to use touch alone, when identifying objects. We showed him a simple lathe (a tool he wished he could use) and he was very excited. We showed it him first in a glass case, at the Science Museum in London, and then we opened the case. With the case closed, he was quite unable to say anything about it, except that the nearest part might be a handle (which it was – the transverse feed handle), but when he was allowed to touch it, he closed his eyes and placed his hand on it when he immediately said with assurance that it was a handle. He ran his hands eagerly over the rest of the lathe, with his eyes tight shut for a minute or so; then he stood back a little, and opening his eyes and staring at it he said: 'Now that I have felt it I can see.'[8]

So also, for instance, a man whose sight had seriously deteriorated had a corneal graft which improved his sight but this is what he wrote subsequent to the operation:

Seeing, which takes place in the brain, not the eye, is the result of the retinal input to the brain, and of learning – mostly unconscious. For twenty years my brain had repeatedly had to re-learn how to deliver the best 'seeing' from diminished retinal input and it had done this impressively well. This time there was an increase of retinal input and, until my brain had done some

> *re-learning, this was confusing so that although what I saw was excitingly different and qualitatively better, for a time, in some ways, I saw worse.*⁹

We learn to see; we learn to suck, we learn to swallow. An analyst was treating a three-year-old who had not learnt to swallow. I have given an instance where a man's capacity to thank had not been learnt and then a case of someone who had to learn to see, then of a child who had not learnt to swallow but there are other functions that also need to be learnt such as the capacity for empathy, the capacity to imagine, the ability to reflect, the ability to think. How are these very fundamental activities learnt? None of the ones I have mentioned are learnt at school; they are not even taught in a conscious way by a child's parents. So the implication here is that in each person there are, in all probability, some aptitudes which have not been learnt.

Rousseau says this very clearly:

> *Man's education begins at birth; before he can speak or understand he is learning. Experience precedes instruction; when he recognizes his nurse he had learnt much. The knowledge of the most ignorant man would surprise us if we had followed his course from birth to the present time. If all human knowledge were divided into two parts, one common to all, the other peculiar to the learned, the latter would seem very small compared to the former.*¹⁰

This truth raises the important question which is 'Can these unlearned activities that have not occurred in babyhood be learnt in later life?' 'In the analytic situation, for instance?' Is this then the analyst's task: 'to engage in such a way that what is empty and unlearned begins to be learnt? And if so, 'how does the analyst need to conduct himself or herself in order that these functions are able to develop?' There is a clue as to the answer that comes from the researches of those who have investigated attachment. I give you this quote from Peter Hobson:

> *The person who is free to evaluate attachments is able to assimilate and <u>think about</u> her own past experiences in relationships, even when these have been unsatisfactory. She has mental space to relate to her own relations with others. She can reflect on her own feelings and impulses and can forgive and tolerate her own shortcomings. So, too, she has space to relate to her own baby as an independent and separate person and to be sensitive to her baby's states of mind in such a way that the baby is likely to become securely attached. . . . A dismissing mother is often restricted in her sensitivity towards her infant, often finding it difficult to be emotionally flexible and responsive. Her infant is likely to respond by becoming avoidant and in some ways controlled in turn.*¹¹

He is saying here that the mother's attitude towards herself, towards her own experiences has an effect upon her baby; that when she is able to reflect on her experiences, even when they have been unsatisfactory, then the child is able to become securely attached. I think the phrase *securely attached* is unsatisfactory and I would replace it by saying that such a baby is *able to relate*. What is implied here in this quote from Peter Hobson's book is that an inner mental act transmits from the mother to the baby.

There is evidence that there can even be transmission of a mental act from the mind of a human being to the mind of an animal. Konrad Lorenz had a parrot which would make a distinct squawk when he was leaving the house but only when he was actually leaving. When he pretended to be leaving the parrot did not squawk. He experimented by putting on a coat and hat as though he were leaving the house but the parrot did not squawk. It was the inner act to which the parrot responded not the outer performance. Konrad Lorenz said that the parrot must have picked up some small subtle clue that told it whether its master was or was not leaving the house. I don't think that Lorenz is right in supposing that the parrot was relying on a subtle clue but that it was the inner act that transmitted to the parrot. Rosenthal tested this with experimental psychologists. He told one group that the rats they were due to observe in a maze were 'genius rats' and to another group he said that the rats were 'stupid' and then each group watched their chosen rats negotiate a maze. The 'genius' rats ran the maze much better and more efficiently than the 'stupid' rats but in fact both lots of rats were of the same generic type; they were neither clever nor stupid. The conclusion seems to be that the mental expectation of the experimental psychologists transmitted to the rats.[12] I believe it is correct that the mental state in one person transmits to another who is in his focus of attention. This is the locus of communication. An interpretation in words enables the memory to categorize a particular communication just as the writing down of a conversation gives it permanence. When someone senses that something being said to him is not true this endorses the truth that this preverbal inner registration is the communicative factor. Therefore that which is transformative for the two participants in the analytic process is the inner imagery, the inner beliefs, the inner attitude and not the words which are their external representation. What Hobson says about the mother in relation to her baby is true also of the analyst in relation to his or her patient. The oft repeated statement that interpretation is the agent of change in psycho-analysis is wrong. What can bring about transformation is the inner imaginative 'pictures' in one that transmits to the other.

Therefore the mental state of the analyst transmits to the patient just as the mother's state transmits to her baby and as the experimenter's state transmits to the animal. So, for instance, some years ago a patient could not pay me at the time of treatment but told me she was able to do so in nine months' time when a sum of money was coming to her. I accepted this and trusted that she would pay as she had promised to do. She was surprised that I trusted her. I would find it difficult to explain why I trusted her. I would not trust everyone or anyone in such a situation. I think I detected an inner attitude that led me to trust her. When I agreed to her proposal and my trust in her honourability she noticed that she began to trust two friends of hers more than she had in the past. So *my* trust of her generated *her* trust in those two friends of hers. So there is a generative power that transmits to the other in such a way that it becomes established in the other. So there are two factors here: the first is that the inner mental state transmits to the other directly and secondly that this can become established in the other in such a way that it becomes part of the other's mental world.

I am careful to distinguish between two individuals and two persons. Two individuals refers to the fact that each one is isolated from the other; two persons, on the other hand, indicates that they are in a shared communion, a shared medium, with each other. The term *person* implies that a single individual is in a shared medium with another. It implies a 'two-ness.' When we use the term *individual* we imply that there is not a shared medium, that there is not a 'two-ness.'

* * *

I have noticed that the presence of a severe super-ego, or even a milder super-ego, is a sign of some undeveloped function within the personality. One might ask therefore why this state is castigated. I think it is that in the animal nature there is a built-in force that eliminates the damaged specimen. Survival of the fittest is at work to produce fully developed and healthy offspring. So it is instinctive that the individual castigates him- or herself for being stupid or ignorant. This is why someone punishes him- or herself for something which is not his or her fault; it is because he, through no fault of his own is being unfaithful to the principle of survival of the fittest and therefore not fair to the next generation. Sometimes this poorly formed entity is not clearly evident because it is often covered with a puffed-up egoism. Omnipotence is very frequently the tell-tale sign that there is a dysfunction within the personality. If the various factors of the mind are working well I have no need to swagger around arrogantly.

Not even the greatest animal lover would claim that an animal, even the apes, are religious. I give you this definition of religion which comes from Engelman who was a friend and fellow philosopher of Wittgenstein:

> *If I am unhappy and know that my unhappiness reflects a gross discrepancy between myself and life as it is, I solved nothing; I shall be on the wrong track and I shall never find a way out of the chaos of my emotions and thoughts so long as I have not achieved the supreme and crucial insight that that discrepancy is not the fault of life as it is, but myself as I am. . . .*
>
> *The person who has achieved this insight and holds on to it, and who will try again and again to live up to it, is religious.*[13]

What therefore religion introduces into the human animal is the fact that there is in humans a principle that transcends the 'survival of the fittest' of the lower animals; that the *quality* of that survival is also of supreme importance. Human beings have always rebelled against tyranny; that there is in all of us a desire for living as free human beings. Human beings have the capacity to choose and when this is seriously restricted then a rebellion gets going. So there are motivating principles that transcend survival, that transcend also the desire to be happy and avoid pain. This is expressed in the quote I have given from John Macmurray. I want therefore to develop a clinical attitude that respects these motivational principles that are governed by attitudes, moral attitudes, that transcend, that go beyond, that go deeper, than the thrust to survive. So I bring clinical examples to throw more light upon the diverse motivations that move us human beings inwardly and outwardly this way and that.

Many patients leave analysis with a super-ego undiminished in its intensity because the fact that it points to a mental dysfunction has not been attended to. As said above it signals the fact that one of these functions responsible for an important mode of acting is poorly developed and that this has not been noted in the analysis. Does this mean that if the ego and all its functions are fully evolved or nearly so, that the super-ego will be only minimally present in the personality? I think this is so. A woman had a very powerful super-ego; she was someone with a very vivid imagination and diverse imagery coloured her inner world but one day it became clear that she was unable to synthesize or integrate these diverse images. When she began to realize this inability to synthesize it was when she was beginning to be able to synthesize. When this occurred it coincided with a significant diminution of the power of her super-ego.

* * *

There is frequently a division of perception within a patient. For instance she will see the analyst quite falsely through one lens but accurately through another. Putting it simply (though not accurately) the super-ego has taken in one way of seeing the analyst and the ego has taken in quite a different one. Again the question is why this is so? Is there any way of acting such that the ego's 'taking-in' becomes dominant and the super-ego's way recedes? So, for instance, I mention above that the super-ego takes in one way and the ego another and yet this is not accurate. In such a group I would want to explore what would be a more accurate way of describing this. Also if one takes it that capacities can be in the personality either through the agency of the super-ego or the ego what are the inner determinants that in the one case drives the individual to use the super-ego agency or what are the circumstances, inner and outer, that enable the ego to be the dominant functioning agency? We shall examine this more closely in the fourth chapter where the focus will be on the hypnotic function that operates in all schools of thinking, religious, scientific and aesthetic.

I believe there is a process which is capable of developing undeveloped functions both in the patient and the analyst. The question is what exactly is the process? It is not sufficient to say 'the psycho-analytic process' because this is too general a statement; a subtle change of emotional attitude can bring about an alteration in the inner happenings of the patient. There had been a psycho-analytic process in progress prior to this subtle change so there is something more distinctive that needs to be understood. I also want to understand the details of the processes that go under the name of projection, projective identification, repression, denial and so on. I throw out these terms with casual ease but I do not truly understand them. For instance I notice often references to feelings being projected but feelings are not projected but are, on the contrary, the registration of a projection . . . if not projection of feelings then what? It is easy to fall back on Bion and say 'Oh *beta elements*'; this is true but what are *beta elements*?

My clinical attention has been for some years on 'deep transferences.' When I use the term 'transference' here I am not referring to an illusory image that is attributed to the analyst. I am referring to illusions that fashion the perception of the world around him or her. These are the sort of illusions I mean: a man believed that he was dead; a woman believed that she would never die; a man believed that when he died the universe would at the same moment come to an end; a woman believed that she did not exist; a man thought all people in the world were figments of his imagination and that he was the only man in the world who did exist; someone else believed that the analyst knew all the details of his life without his having to tell the analyst, another thought the other individual in the room with him was an extension of himself . . . and so on. I give all of these illusory beliefs the generic term: *ostensible illusion*. People frequently say such transference illusions are only so of people who are very disturbed. My experience is that this is not so; that people who come complaining of some mild ailment often have transference illusions like these operating in them; that the 'mild ailment' points to one of these serious aberrations deep down in the personality. When such illusions are operating they affect the way such an individual relates to others and his or her whole way of navigating his or her way through life. This perspective gets aborted when what the patient is saying is moulded into an interpretation about the way the patient is perceiving the analyst. It consciously restricts the arena of disturbance from psychotic to neurotic. It is at the neurotic level that someone distils the shape of an entity, the shape of an individual, whether it be mother, sibling or analyst. But this misses the deeper beliefs that I am naming *ostensible illusions*. I give detailed examples of such transferences; trying to understand how such delusions have formed themselves and whether such delusions can dissipate and, if so, how. I elaborate the significance of *ostensible illusions* more fully in the penultimate lecture. So you will have to be patient!

Connected is the way in which these deep transferences are kept in being through 'magical acts.' I look at these and catalogue the different forms they take and how these also initiate damaging or annihilating mental states. When the individual is merged within a group belief, then his or her own knowledge is smothered and personhood is strangled and prevented from coming to birth. The individual is still in a state of foetal development. How has this occurred? What is the process that has not happened in childhood for this person? What is it that has hampered the journey into adulthood? Can the failed process be re-awakened in adulthood? And can it happen within the analytic process? What elements in the analytic process need to be accentuated? And which need to be diminished?

These illusions which I have just enumerated are always brought into being by a 'magical act.' This is an inner psychological act that brings the illusion into being. The act is constructed out of two elements: first a negative hallucination that wipes out the reality that is there and then the construction of the *ostensible illusion*. Sometimes the *ostensible illusion* is there permanently. Usually this seems to be the case but there is a mode of action from another that is able to dispel it. It is always kept in being if the other person is also subject to an illusion. The latter may not be as obviously erroneous as the *ostensible illusion* but nevertheless it shares two of its components. Examination of this process will include an analysis of 'magical acts.'

* * *

In this book there is also an investigation into what is known as 'the unconscious.' In much writing it is thought that the realm of the mind referred to as unconscious is the same as consciousness but not attended to or noted. Freud said that there are no feelings in the unconscious so he knew the unconscious arena of the mind is not the same as the area of consciousness. It is because they are in a totally different mode that they are unconscious. Feelings are one aspect of awareness, of consciousness. Awareness and consciousness are synonyms. It is also true not that there is a thought but it happens to be unconscious but rather that there is no such thing as a thought in this realm. Therefore the unconscious refers to a state in the personality that is almost totally different from what we know in consciousness. It is unconscious because the agglomerative mass is in some undifferentiated and indistinguishable state. So we attempt to understand better what this state is like and how we can think about it. My belief is that the better we understand it, the more its structure changes. The act of understanding has a transformative function. The perspicacious intuition in one person fosters a creative change in another.

So these are the investigations that are the substance of this book. If at any point this rings a bell and you find yourself saying 'That's just what I keep wondering about' or that it stimulates other enquiries not mentioned here then pursue your search in the direction that beckons you. My own experience is that exploring and pushing further one's understanding is illuminating for clinical work but also gives enlightening insights into our culture with all its values and institutional forms.

Notes

1 Mcneile Dixon, W. (1958). *The Human Situation*. p. 175. Penguin Books.
2 Berlin, I. (1979). *Against the Current*. London: The Hogarth Press.
3 Newman, J.H. (1927). *The Idea of a University*. p. 134. New York, London, Toronto, Bombay & Calcutta: Longmans, Green & Co.
4 Freud, S. (1930). *Civilization and Its Discontents*. S.E. v. XXI. p. 76. London: The Hogarth Press & The Institute of Psycho-Analysis.

5 Macmurray, John (1949). *Conditions of Freedom.* p. 2. Toronto: The Ryerson Press.
6 Berlin, Isaiah (1979). *Against the Current.* [The Counter-Enlightenment]. p. 8. London: The Hogarth Press.
7 Mcneile Dixon, W. (1958). *The Human Situation.* p. 63. Penguin Books.
8 Gregory, R.L. (1967). *Eye and Brain.* pp. 197–198. World University Library. London: Weidenfeld and Nicolson.
9 Mann, Peter and Sargy Mann. (2008). *Sargy Mann.* p. 162. SP Books.
10 Rousseau, Jean-Jacques (2013). *Emile.* p. 33. Mineola, NY: Dover Publications.
11 Hobson, Peter (2002). *The Cradle of Thought.* p. 178. London: Palgrave Macmillan.
12 Koestler, Arthur (1976). *The Act of Creation.* p. 568. London: Hutchinson & Co. (Danube Edition). Viz: Rosenthal, R. and K. L. Fode (1963). The Effect of Experimenter Bias on the Performance of the Albino Rat. *Behavioral Science*, VIII, 3 July.
13 Monk, Ray (1990). *Ludwig Wittgenstein.* p. 185. New York, Oxford, Singapore & Sydney: The Free Press & Maxwell Macmillan.

Chapter 1

The core of the personality

The core of the personality is a creator. This is a simple statement but it goes counter to the way this core is presented both in psycho-analytic discourse and within the social sciences more generally. This core of the personality is frequently referred to as a bunch of instinctual drives with the ego or self 'managing' them. I give this quote from Arnold Toynbee because he is warning against the scientific attitude that turns living things into inanimate objects. Consider this statement of Freud:

> *the ego is especially under the influence of perception, and that, speaking broadly, perceptions may be said to have the same significance for the ego as instincts have for the id. At the same time the ego is subject to the influence of the instincts, too, like the id, of which it is, as we know, only a specially modified part.*[1]

The ego, in this formulation is slave-like to sensations coming from without and from the instincts that come from within. Instincts are central in Freud's conception of the personality and they, these instincts, are in the service of survival. The struggle for survival, according to this view, is the prime motivating principle in human beings. There is no notion here of some other motive that might compete against this push for survival. It is often thought that rigid belief systems are the preserve of religion but this is wrong. Science is riddled with belief systems and because it is widely believed that this is not so it makes it more difficult to see these systems and the outline that circumscribes them. This notion that Science is free of delusional belief systems is one of the greatest fallacies that courses through scientific discourse like a raging epidemic.

Drives, according to Freud's metapsychology and nearly all thinkers within the Social Sciences, are the foundation of the personality but this is because there is a failure to conceptualize what life is; what defines life. G.K. Chesterton said that it is only the obvious things that are never seen.[2] It is also this tendency to categorize something under a particular system of thinking that distorts what is there. When Science, with its truly enormous advances in the last hundred years, became so dominant that the principles governing the behaviour of matter became applied to everything in the universe including that which was not material. What differentiates something living from something that is inanimate is that in the latter any movement or action that occurs is due to the impact upon it from an outer agent whereas in a living being there is a source of action which comes entirely from within. The percentage of activity that comes from this interior source and what comes from outer impact varies. What comes from within the organism may only be one percent of the total movement or much greater than one percent but what makes it a living being is that at least some of the active movement finds its source entirely within the organism. Inanimate matter has no such source of action from within.

One such belief is that the struggle for survival is what primarily motivates human beings. A characteristic of any belief system is that although there is evidence of instances that belie that system yet these are not seen. A belief always blinds the believer to truths which are inconsistent with the belief. Beliefs are always over simplistic; there is a refusal in them to embrace the complexity of life and its contradictions. In the introduction I quoted Isaiah Berlin who emphasized this.[3] A person who commits suicide is not motivated for his or her survival. Also people giving their lives for an ideological belief and patriotism for instance, especially in the case of a war, is a motive that governs myriads of people rather than the thrust for survival. It is also so that people with a great passion for music, for poetry, for ornithology often place these affections of the heart more highly than the conservation of their life. Pasteur, for instance, dedicated his life to the investigation and study of bacteria. Of course he needed to be alive; he had to eat and drink and have shelter. This was necessary just as gravity is necessary to prevent me floating off into the air. Gravity and the thrust for survival are the planetary conditions for the different modes of existence upon Planet Earth. They are not the guide posts for the individual's personal direction in life. Pasteur created his vocational direction.

I stress this survival motive because it is the underlying assumption in nearly all thinking within the Social Sciences and thus the instincts are thought to be the ground rocks within the personality. Yet we know that we would not see the world as it is if there had been no Buddha, no Socrates, no Aristotle, no Moses, no Jesus, no Augustine, no Muhammad, no Moses Maimonides, no Aquinas, no Leonardo de Vinci, no Descartes, no Spinoza, no Tolstoy and so on. Yet with what was it that these individuals endowed our world? Something entirely unbidden moved inside of each of these human beings; something that came entirely from within them. They were not pressured in any way to go in a direction which they had been ordered to follow. An inner something rose up inside of them that was stimulated from nowhere. It came entirely from within them and it was not governed by the need to survive. The passion to give an explanation, the idea that this has caused that, is that the mind cannot face the shocking truth that something has arisen entirely from within with no external stimulus to explain it. Just as God had to be produced to explain the world so also 'explanation' is produced to hide from us that scandal of the mind: that something has no source outside of itself.

Humans are animals and, in our animality, there is a thrust for survival. This survival-push is a characteristic of all objects in the universe: it is a something that demands the integrity of the object. A stone of a particular size and shape has a principle of conservation within it. When a stone-maker takes an axe and hacks a huge granite rock into small cubic shapes to make his pavé road he is going counter to the original rock's quiddity of substance. It is the same with an organism. It has in it a principle of conservation but in the case of an organism it requires particular elements to be ingested from outside its circumference to sustain it. This need for elements from outside to be taken within, in order to sustain it, is what differentiates a living organism from entities that are inanimate. There are two different modes of taking in. One is the minute to minute taking in of oxygen and the expulsion of carbon dioxide and the other is the taking in of food and water, some of which is expelled in faeces and urine. All living things, except human beings, are ruled by this principle of conservation. In a human being there is a central principle that is able to and does, in certain circumstances, defy this principle. What I am referring to here is that a human being can choose to kill him- or herself, can choose to put his or her passion for art as a guiding principle rather than be governed by the principle of conservation, can decide to do something for the sake of another instead of being governed by the principle of conservation or can decide, as the monk, to renounce his sexual desires in favour of a dedication to God. Someone may decide to go to war and put his or her life at risk. It is this capacity of the human being to release him- or herself from the generalized instinct governing his or her animality that differentiates him or her from the lower animals. The Russian thinker, Vladimir Soloviev, characterized that which was specifically human according to three principles: shame, pity and reverence. What lies behind shame is a presence within the personality of an entity that is able to observe the activity of the personality. The product of this inner entity is awareness or consciousness. What is this entity, this presence, that produces this awareness? There is in human beings, in their animality, this thrust for survival but also a creator that is free of this struggle for survival and, not only free, but capable of a strength that is greater than the survival struggle. The philosopher, John Macmurray, a much underappreciated recent thinker, emphasizes that there are occasions when someone will over-ride the impulse for survival and be prepared even to sacrifice his or her life. I quoted Macmurray in the introduction but will, for the sake of emphasis, quote it again:

> *Freedom is, I am assured, the pearl of great price for which, if we are wise, we shall be prepared to sell all our possessions, to buy it. The ancient and widespread belief that the supreme good of human life is happiness – for all its persuasiveness – is false. Freedom has a higher value than happiness; and this is what we recognize when we honour those who have been ready to sacrifice happiness, and even life itself, for freedom's sake.*[4]

What Macmurray implies is that a person may and sometimes does sacrifice his or her very life for the sake of freedom. It means that freedom has a value that transcends the thrust for survival; and freedom is possible because the core of the personality is a creator. If the ego is not a creator there is no freedom. Psychoanalysis is rooted in the belief that the struggle for survival is the dominant motivational principle and the servants of this are the instincts or the drives. That the struggle for survival is *a* motivational principle is definitely so but that it is the prime and only purpose in people's lives is false.

There is a game that used to be played when I was a child. I, or another child, was blindfolded and then led up to a table upon which were twenty different objects. I was told to feel each of the objects and then say what they were. A typical array of objects chosen might be: a potato, a screwdriver, a cigarette lighter, an orange, a crucifix, a diary, a camera, a paint brush, a potato peeler, a cork, an ashtray, a puzzle-box, a Yale key, the model of a ship, an acorn, a kitchen weighing machine, a film for a camera, a hardboiled egg and a thimble. It might be thought that it would be easy for the blindfolded person to guess correctly what these different objects were when they could be felt by touch but not seen. In fact it was difficult and many incorrect guesses occurred which would always evoke laughter. What is happening here? I take it that I know through vision those objects just mentioned. How do I *know* that what I see there is a hardboiled egg? In fact sight alone will not tell me this. If, however, I see a salad being served up for lunch and next to it are some eggs I *assume* that they are hard boiled and not raw and uncooked. I *assume* it from the context. If however I knew that this person serving up the lunch is a well-known practical joker I might be more cautious and not make this assumption. What I am doing when using my imagination in this game is to categorize each object. Here is a single object that I am feeling by touch with my hands and I am being asked to put it into the right folder in the filing cabinet. Screwdrivers, cigarette lighters, oranges, crucifixes and diaries are all generalities. Feeling by touch is of an individual object. Vision is, together with hearing, the most generalized of the senses. Vision merges into a concept. So I am being asked in this game to place what is individual into a generalized category. It might be thought that this is easy but in fact a difficult transformation is occurring. I am being asked to put an individual object of a particular shape and size that I can feel with my fingers into a class that includes this single object that I am feeling into an unfelt category. If I feel this oval object and then proclaim that it is an egg I am moving it out of its individual existence that I have been feeling into a concept that is constructed not by the imagination but by an act of intellect. This requires a further elaboration of the mind. Central to this book is the statement that the core of the mind is a creator but just as in the external world there are different products issuing from this creator like paintings, sculpture, poetry and music so also this creator is able to fashion mental realities that are detached from the senses, or at least detached from the tactile senses. As already stated vision is the sense that is furthest removed from the tactile. If I see a creature walking across the lawn and ask what it is I am told that it is a tortoise. 'Oh I see' I reply. I had already seen the animal visually so when I say 'Oh I see' I am using a visual analogy for a mental concept that I have created. So imagination here is servant to conceptual demand. This is one mode in which imagination functions but it is the lowest. It is here servant to reasoning. The base of reasoning is the intellect placing visual objects into generalized categories and imagination is being used to assist in the enterprise.

Imagination is the creator's instrument so it can be used in the service of categorizing just explained but it can also be used to give communication to itself. I give this quote from Collingwood:

> Some people have thought that a poet who wishes to express a great variety of subtly differentiated emotions might be hampered by the lack of a vocabulary rich in words referring to the distinctions between them; and that psychology by working out such a vocabulary, might render a valuable service to poetry. This is the opposite of the truth. The poet needs no such words at all; the existence or non-existence of a scientific terminology describing the emotions he wishes to express is to him a matter of perfect indifference. If such a terminology, where it exists, is allowed to affect his own use of language, it affects it for the worse.
>
> The reason why description, so far from helping expression, actually damages it, is that description generalizes. To describe a thing is to call it a thing of such and such a kind; to bring it under a conception, to classify it. Expression, on the contrary, individualizes. The anger which I feel here and now, with a certain person, for a certain cause, is no doubt an instance of anger, and in describing it as anger one is telling the truth about it; but it is much more than mere anger: it is a peculiar anger, not quite like any anger that I ever felt before, and probably not quite like any anger I shall ever feel again. To become fully conscious of it means becoming conscious of it not merely as an instance of anger, but as this quite peculiar anger. Expressing it, we saw, has something to do with becoming conscious of it; therefore, if being fully conscious of it means being conscious of all its peculiarities, fully expressing it means expressing all its peculiarities. The poet, therefore, in proportion as he understands his business, gets as far away as possible from merely labelling his emotions as instances of this or that general kind, and takes enormous pains to individualize them by expressing them in terms which reveal their difference from any other emotion of the same sort.[5]

A good example of this can be seen by studying Shelley's poem *The Skylark*. The lark flies higher and higher and the unpoetical generalizer says 'until the bird is out of sight' but let us listen to the poet. He says

> *The pale purple even*
> *Melts around thy flight.*

The sheer beauty of Shelley's image is breathtaking. As Collingwood says no constructor of verbiage, psychological or social, could offer Shelley a helping hand; in fact he would be throwing a hand grenade into the poet's assembly of fancy. The creator assigns here to imagination its most precious gem: the making of beauty.

* * *

I have emphasized that actions that flow from the core of the mind, the creative centre, expand and deepen the mind but there is an implication here that there are actions which do not originate in this creative centre. There are entities within the mind which frequently smother this inner core and many actions flow from these alien implants. The question that naturally arises is how do these obstructive aliens become implanted in the personality? It is necessary to formulate the notion that each human being is surrounded by a protective membrane. Freud referred to this as a *stimulus barrier* and described it in *Beyond the Pleasure Principle*. He was confronted with this when soldiers in the First World War were shell shocked which meant that the explosion of a shell nearby imploded into the inner world of the soldier who was nearby and this led to a repetitive series of unplanned actions. The implosion into the inner world of foreign elements leads to actions which are not governed by any creative action from within. The way Freud envisions the *stimulus barrier* is by seeing it as if it were a heavy raincoat that kept out the rain and hail from pelting down upon the body. He saw an organism with this protective membrane around it. In particular he saw its prime role as not so much to let in stimuli but rather to keep out stimuli which were disturbing to the focus of attention. He says:

> *Protection against stimuli is an almost more important function for the living organism than reception of stimuli . . . the sense organs, which consist essentially of apparatus for the reception of certain specific effects of stimulation, but which also include special arrangements for further protection against excessive amounts of stimulation and for excluding unsuitable kinds of stimuli.*[6]

Each human being is enveloped by a membrane which allows in stimuli from the surrounding environment and also keeps out stimuli that interfere with the object which is engaging the individual's attention. Freud named this membrane the *stimulus barrier*. He emphasized, as this quote makes clear, that its capacity to prevent stimuli from entering was probably more important than its function of letting stimuli in.

The term 'stimulus barrier' or 'membrane' harmonize with the model of a human being as an organism but as the thesis of this book is that the core of the personality is a creative agent, an important function of which is to keep out stimuli that it cannot process and only give entry to those that it can, so the image of a chef who selects the right ingredients to make beef stroganoff and rejects those that are unsuitable is an analogy that fits better with our conceptualization of the personality. It is the idea here that a constituent of this inner core is the capacity to choose and differentiate. Therefore it can choose to admit this stimulus but refuse that one. He also makes the point that this membrane has a differentiating function. It is able to diagnose the difference between harmful stimuli and those that are beneficial.

We can however keep the term 'membrane' as long as it is clear that this is a function under the governance of the creative core. It's that the core is the creator of the membrane. So when a patient said that her membrane was too porous I take the view that the creative core has not fashioned the membrane in a mode that is beneficial for her. It has been fashioned not according to her desires, the desires of this particular person but rather according to the desires or outlook of someone else; maybe her father or her mother or an institution of which she is a member.

* * *

We tend, when we think of traumatic happenings in someone's life, to think immediately of a bad-tempered father who shouted or hit his children, a mother who was cruel and made her children eat food so hot that it burned their tongues. We can think of many other versions of hateful behaviour; of a mother who told her child she hated him; of a father who put his fingers up the vagina of his four-year-old daughter. What is more difficult to picture clearly is the disaster when something is *not* given, a something, an ingredient, which was hungered for but *not* forthcoming. In the sixth chapter I refer to capacities in relation to the self and also capacities in relation to the Other. In some ways these two categories should not be distinguished on the basis of self and other because the other is effected by the capacities in relation to the self. So, for instance, Hobson says that a child, whose mother is not able to reflect on her own experiences, is unable to attach securely:

> *The person who is free to evaluate attachments is able to assimilate and <u>think about</u> her own past experiences in relationships, even when these have been unsatisfactory. She has mental space to relate to her own relations with others. She can reflect on her own feelings and impulses and can forgive and tolerate her own shortcomings. So, too, she has space to relate to her own baby as an independent and separate person and to be sensitive to her baby's states of mind in such a way that the baby is likely to become securely attached.*[7]

This is a very striking statement because the mother is not doing this so that her baby can attach securely but nevertheless this personal activity has this very salutary effect on the baby. We need to stretch this more widely to include not just the mother in relation to her baby but any one person in relation to another. It is the inner activity that holds the power. I will give you an example.

A man in his thirties, named Timothy, was emotionally crippled that prevented him from working, from making relationships. He had an eye for pretty girls and longed to have one of them as his girl-friend but they constantly rejected him. He came into a session. He said,

> *I feel completely hopeless. I had cherished a hope that I could get better, that I could be normal like other people but now I feel totally hopeless.*

I sat there knowing that there were no words that could give him a sympathy for his despair or alleviate it. So I sat in silence. Then an unexpected thing happened. Memory images began to pass across the screen of my mind – memories when I had felt totally hopeless, that nothing could alleviate the gloom and one particular image came across the inner screen – when I was walking down a drab London road with a case in my hand with a few paltry belongings and having no idea where I was to go. Quite uninvited this scene came before me with a fierce intensity. I let it pass before me and I watched and then two or three other scenes from the same era passed across the inner radar. I had forgotten what it was like to feel totally at a loss and without hope in the world. I said nothing but let this cinematic performance inside of me happen. These things had happened to me but now they were alive and vivid. The silence slid on for five or ten minutes. Then he said,

> *Last week a girl I'd love to go out with turned to me and said 'Timothy I like you and would like to see you again.'*

That incident came to him. He had forgotten it. He felt a glimmer of hope. My being with him in the abyss of hopelessness gave him a glint of hope. There is a passageway between the inner mental acts of one to that of the other. If this is so then it means that interpretation, the putting into words, is not the prime agent of change in psycho-analysis. The prime agent is the *inner* mental acts of the analyst. So the self-reflection of the mother has a good consequence for her baby. What was it that was occurring in myself in the clinical vignette that I have just given? It was a dream-memory of my own. When I use the term 'dream-memory' I do not mean that it was not an actual happening that had occurred but rather the fact that the memory of past events in my own life were not consciously looked for but they came, as if unbidden, across the visual screen of my mind. But when I say 'unbidden' it does not mean there was no trigger that produced them. The trigger was clearly Timothy's despair which triggered a despair of my own; this was not a present despair for me but one from forty years previously which, though so long ago, was still in me. This suggests that togetherness in a shared experience is the healing agent. Yet one has to diagnose this carefully. There is nothing here of 'Let us be together in our misery' but rather that what is healing is a knowledge that is not abstract but personal and that this kind of knowledge transmits without words. This way of thinking has made it clear to me that interpretation is not, of itself, the agent of change but rather what brings about change is an inner energy whose source is in a personal experience. Inner states of this kind transmit to the other. In this last sentence the words *of this kind* are essential to define and diagnose. Why was it that Timothy's despair cued into a despair of my own? I think it is that an inner state is never individual, just individual. It is here that interpretation – the putting into words – of an experience tells us something. A word or phrase used to describe something has a meaning and a meaning is, in its essential nature, something whose source is in a commonality. There would have been no point in Timothy speaking of his hopelessness if he thought I would not understand what he was talking of. He knows when he speaks of hopelessness that I know what hopelessness is or otherwise there would be no point in his referring to it. But me, as the recipient of this message, can receive it in one of two ways: either as an abstract entity or as a personal one. A sign that it is being received in an abstract way is indicated when the clinician starts to speak about hopelessness, a speech in which he sympathizes with Timothy's state. The other is to allow Timothy's state to generate an equivalent state in the clinician. Hopelessness is a shared state; if it were not there would be no word for it. Timothy's hopelessness meets up with my hopelessness. The characteristic of the dream state, reverie, free-floating attention or a wide-unfocussed stare is active: it seeks out the equivalent state in the other. This activity can be thwarted by an intervention coming from a place of supposed scientific enquiry. There is, as Marion Milner says, quoting Elton Mayo, directed thinking and undirected thinking.[8] It is dream-life, undirected thinking, that is the source of poetry. Poetry flows from, out of, this dream-like mood. Poetry is its expression. Those great poets whom we all admire – Shakespeare, Coleridge, Shelley, Keats – had this capacity developed to a high degree and were able to find the right coloured language and rhythm to express it.

The statement here is that what is healing of mental disorder is shared experience. Let us look at this more searchingly. What is psychosis? Frequently, when being explained, substitute words are given for psychosis like primitive, archaic or primordial but these are just alternative terms. They do not define what it is. These terms all refer to something that is yet unformed and in this they do touch on an element of the condition known as psychosis but it is peripheral, not its essence. What constitutes psychosis is the emotional state of isolation and this is why a *shared experience* is the medicine of healing. There is some background necessary to understand isolation properly. It is not the same as loneliness. A central theme of this book is that the core of the personality is creative; that it is from this core that we find our bearings in life. Consider this statement of Arnold Toynbee:

> *The heart longs to be given its bearings in the mysterious and formidable Universe in which it finds itself; and the higher religions have responded to this longing by issuing what purport to be authoritative and precise directions.*[9]

He says that the heart longs *to be given* its bearings rather than find bearings for itself. This statement of Toynbee implies a certain passivity in the face of the wide range of possibilities. 'Show me the way' comes a cry from the heart. Toynbee goes on to say:

> *The Judaic religions claim to be able to tell us just where we stand in the no-man's land between the first year of the World and the last; the Buddha claims*

> to be able to tell us just what we have to do in order to make our exit into Nirvana. These unverified and unverifiable claims obtain our assent because we are eager to give it. This eagerness is a natural reaction to our awkward human condition. None the less, our deliberate credulity is an infirmity which we ought to resist. . . . It is a mistake – and this a moral as well as an intellectual one – to take on trust, from an <u>ipse dixit</u>, confident answers to fundamental questions that human minds find themselves unable to answer for themselves, even by the utmost exertion of their inborn intellectual powers.[10]

He emphasizes here that to find our own way requires the *utmost exertion* and yet he is recommending it. We immediately think of religions when we start considering 'guides for living' but there are many secular versions of this. Communism immediately comes to mind but there are many others like Behaviourism, Atheism, Agnosticism, Vitalism, Determinism, Economic Rationalism or Psychoanalysis. Each of these suggest to the individual that he or she attach him- or herself to the dictates of the particular doctrine in question. The state of undirected thinking requires an executioner's detachment from any dictate arising from a religious or secular jurisdiction. This is what Bion meant when he recommended a state *without memory or desire.*

* * *

The functioning of the creative core depends to a large extent upon the respectful freedom given to the individual. So the mother of Stephen noticed that he tapped with a metal spoon six empty milk bottles. She then put different quantities of water in each bottle and so when her son tapped them on a subsequent occasion there was a different note emitted from each. 'He has a musical ear,' she said to herself and bought him a mouth organ which he began to play with patience and stamina. That story ends by Stephen going to the Consortium for Music and ended by becoming the lead violinist in a national orchestra. Another son of the same mother became a first rate mathematician. This mother attended in a tuned way to the aspirations of her children and thus fostered the desires of their hearts. In this way she 'fecundated' the appetites of their hearts in the way that Coleridge, according to Francis Thompson, did to a number of poets.[11]

What is it that leads one person to become an historian, another a painter, another an engineer, another a musician, another an aviator, another a geologist? What inner stewardship leads one person in this direction and someone else in a different one? That there is talent that favours one particular career must be one aspect of it but there is something else. There is desire that moves **him** in one direction and **her** in another. Desire is a component part of the creative core. Desire is what gives force and impetus to the chosen vocation. But how is it that desire is of one colour in this person and of a different hue in another? Sometimes the son follows the father but sometimes son or daughter strike out in a completely different direction. Why does this one have a passion for music while this other one is dedicated to ornithology? An Australian aviatrix, Nancy Bird, knew from the age of four that she wanted to be a pilot.[12] Clearly she could only have such a desire if she lived in an age and location where there were planes. If she had been born in the eighteenth century this would not have been possible. So the social world into which someone is born has an inviting influence. So there has to be this outer object that sends out an invitation that is accepted by this one but not the other one. But what it is that draws Michael towards being a chef and Margaret to being a travel writer? This is the conundrum for which no answer is forthcoming. It requires the recognition of *mystery*. *Mystery*, properly understood, means that the human mind is limited in its capacity to grasp that which differentiates one person from another but it is also that the inner mindset goes in one direction rather than another. We have already given voice to this dilemma in the Introduction. The aim here is to focus upon that which limits the human capacity.

We have to posit a harmony of sentiment between the individual and the direction in which he or she decides to navigate his or her life. Augustine of Hippo said that we become what we love. When we use the above terms: historian, painter, engineer, musician, aviator or geologist we are talking of people who are bound in their 'work-path' to a particular investigation into one aspect of the world. So when someone wants to be one of these objects, one of these chosen fields, he or she feels him- or herself together with historians or painters or engineers. It seems that this is already in him or her and he or she wants to develop it. It means there is some knowledge of the inner aspiration but also there is a commonality in the person between her and a particular group of others. The historian or engineer is already there and known to be there. There is an appetite for this rather than that. There is some knowledge that it is not possible to be everything. So there is knowledge in the individual of limitation. I have to choose one of these. 'I am a limited creature so although I should love to be an historian, a painter, an engineer, a musician, an aviator and a geologist I am forced to give myself to one of these and renounce the others.' In adolescence the individual frequently wants all at once. So, on the arrival of adulthood, there comes to me a knowledge of the wide variety of professional careers and, at the same time, a knowledge that to give of myself and become an *aficionado* in any one means making a choice and limiting myself to one pathway. We might say that adulthood is that state in which recognition, practical recognition, is known and embraced. This choice seems to be dictated by aptitude and talent. If I am useless at mathematics I will probably not be drawn to becoming an engineer and if I have no talent for drawing or painting I am unlikely to become a painter but maybe I have an interest in my parents' lives and my grandparents' so then I am drawn to becoming an historian. What prompts that inner vocation is mysterious.

This chapter is on how the individual is restricted in the face of this enormous pageantry of the human scene, so the focus is upon what restricts the individual in his or her own engagement with it. It does seem that there is a kind of sympathy between this individual and one aspect of the world. Why is this person interested in birds, this one drawn to study the stars and this other one the history of the Roman Empire? We do not know but it seems that there is a something in the planetary concourse that exercises attraction upon the souls of individuals. One might call it a higher appetite, taking an analogy from taste. Foods of one kind attract this individual, foods of another attract someone different. So also this same appetitive quality operates in the higher levels of psychic connection with the variety existing in the universe.

* * *

In order to illustrate the power of the inner creator I will tell the story of a painter who went totally blind. Now one would think that painting would be at an end for him. After all one paints what one can see but I can best explain how this 'obvious' conclusion was not how things turned out. I knew this painter well and had known him for thirty years and then in the year 2006 a mutual friend told me that he had gone completely blind so I wrote to him saying how sorry I was that this had happened and I imagined though did not say it that his painting career was at an end. In answer to my letter, which his wife, Frances, had read to him, he wrote back telling me that he had had an exhibition and he wrote the following about it:

My exhibition went incredibly well and I sold all but two of the oils and several gouaches. It was certainly partly as a result of all the publicity I got. I was on Midweek on Radio 4 with Libby Purves and the gallery had twelve enquiries in the first hour and a half after the programme. I suppose it is pretty surprising that I am able to go on painting now that I am totally blind but now that I have been doing it for a year and a half, I take it for granted. What is really wonderful for me is how good my painting chums, and the buying public, bless them, think that these new, blind paintings are. People have actually said that they think that this was my best show to date, how can that be? Since finishing the Cadaques subjects I have been painting Frances sitting in one of two chairs in my studio, a large arm chair and one of those ubiquitous plastic garden chairs which I have put on a table so that I am looking across at Frances rather than down on her. I position myself very close so that I can understand how she is sitting by touch but I have also devised a system of measuring using my white stick so as to work out what she would look like from where I am. I then mark positions on my canvas with little blobs of Blutac – at present about 60 on a painting – so that I know where I am by feel. One of the great innovations is that since I have no perception of light or colour, I can make things any colour I like. These paintings have a simple but much more highly coloured design so that in one I might make the chair bright red and then in the next, I make it green. Likewise the background can be any colour I choose. I paint Frances a natural colour and only paint her clothes colours that she wears, mostly black therefore. Again, the funny thing is that chaps seems to think that these paintings are very good and the living painter I most revere, Leon Kossoff, was so complimentary that I almost wept. So as you can see, Neville, things are going fine and there is definitely life after blindness and a jolly good life at that.

About a year later I was in London and per chance I was present on the opening day of his second exhibition so I saw several of his *blind paintings* and I truly thought they were remarkable. He was there and I heard him speaking to a friend saying that he thought that these paintings were so good because they were in no way derivative of other painters. This was in the year 2008 and at this exhibition there was a book about him produced by the joint effort of himself and his son, Peter. In this book he makes this point:

> *I think that one reason why great figurative painters are different, why a Titian is not like a Piero della Francesca or, a Matisse is not like Cézanne, is because each artist has had to find his own way of harnessing his skills and his temperament, his feelings and his intellect.*[13]

He died on Easter Sunday 2015. Between 2008 and his death I saw him several times: sometimes in London at my club and other times when I visited him in his own home. After he died his wife put together in a short monograph some of his remarkable statements.[14] There follows some of them:

> *with one painting, I thought, I don't want to paint the chair that dark brown I will do what I did some years ago and cover it with a white cloth, then as I was taking the cloth from the cupboard I thought 'you silly bugger you can't see it anyway – you can paint the chair any colour you like.' This was, for me, an astonishingly liberating breakthrough and from that moment on I started using colours in a much more intuitive and decorative way.*[15]

A little bit further on he says:

> *I certainly would never have chosen blindness but the extraordinary paradox is that going blind has taught me to see more and differently, it has taken me somewhere new and exciting, and I have been thrilled to discover that I can make paintings without sight, and that this activity is far more like a continuation of my previous painting experience than I could possibly have imagined.*[16]

A bit further on he says:

> *I've wondered long and hard why the paintings I've made since being totally blind are as good as they are, and indeed, quite a lot of people think they're the best things I've ever done. When my sight was relatively normal – I mean it was never normal, but I could go along to galleries and look at paintings – I think probably I was always a bit on the timid side. I think I was too influenced by the masters I revered, and it's not so much that I was ever influenced by their language, their way of doing it, because I absolutely knew that was a catch. I think what I probably was too influenced by was their vision, their*

experience, and I think that when I went out to choose a subject, in a sort of way I was choosing a version of Monet's subject or Bonnard's subject rather than my own, and when I started going seriously blind that option of going out and finding Monet's subject wasn't there, and because I was so thrown back on my own limitations, curiously, I think this led me into a much more personal world, a world that was more my experience and my way of responding to it.[17]

When this painter friend, Sargy Mann, says here that he was too influenced by the vision of great painters exactly the same can be said of psychotherapists and psycho-analysts. We are too influenced by our revered masters such as Freud, Jung, Klein, Winnicott or Bion. Marion Milner had a friend who was a very perceptive art critic who looked at one of her paintings and I will give you what she says about his judgement of her painting:

after many years of writing, I had finally found people to teach me who did see that the essence of painting is that every mark on the paper should be one's own, growing out of the uniqueness of one's own psycho-physical structure and experience, not a mechanical copy of the model, however skilful. Incidentally I showed this book to a painter, who, while turning over the pages to look at the drawings said, 'That one is not you, nor that, nor that, they are unconscious copies of some picture you have seen.' I had myself recognized the obvious derivation of 'Mrs. Punch' from the Duchess in Alice's Adventures in Wonderland, just as the chair in 'Nursery' derived from van Gogh; and also that the design in the 'Blasting Witch' was a close unconscious copy of the design of a picture I had often seen in a friend's room. But the painter had never seen this friend's picture and it was a surprise to me that anyone could know, without having seen the 'copy,' that the line of the drawing was not my own, not growing out of my own psycho-physical rhythms. Of the wavy line at the top left side of 'The Eagle and the Cave-man' he said, 'That is good, that is from you; though the shading is not, that is mannered, banal.' The point of view prompting these criticisms confirmed my growing conviction that a work of art, whatever its content, or subject, whether a recognizable scene or object or abstract pattern, must be an externalization, through its shapes and lines and colours, of the unique psycho-physical rhythm of the person making it. Otherwise it will have no life in it whatever, for there is no other source of life.[18]

She is saying here that what she painted when 'blind' to the paintings of others, that only then was she able to produce something unique to her. It was even more true with Sargy Mann who actually went blind but then what he painted came entirely out of his own inner core. Marion Milner says that the painting needs to be an externalization of the unique rhythm of the person making it. What happened to Sargy Mann, the blind painter, 'proves' what Marion Milner says. He was no longer slave either to the vision of other painters but also not even to the world of colours as they are impressed upon us when we look with our eyes at a landscape. What he had managed to achieve was to reach through to his inner creator without any obstruction.

What is being said here of painters is also true for the 'painting-language' of psycho-analysts. Only those interpretations that come entirely from within reach through to the psychotic patient or the psychotic arena in every patient. Psychotic patients recognize that which comes from the creative core of the analyst and that which does not. A psycho-analyst in London was having difficulty with a patient so went to consult a supervisor who helped him understand better and then he saw his patient the next day and delivered an interpretation, derived in part from his supervisor's insight. The next day the patient told the analyst that he had had a dream in the night in which he saw the analyst walking down the road towards him. 'But,' he said, it was strange you had on a suit of clothes that was too big for you.'

So my conviction is that the core of the personality is a creator; that the ego, the self, the I, the me, is a creator. But to get past all the obstructions which prevent one from reaching one's own creator is not easy.

The importance of this is that the individual in his/her core may be striving to become who they are but they may have ingested beliefs from the culture which do not truly belong to the core self. I quote to you this snippet from an interview by Ramona Koval with the novelist, David Mitchell:

> *R.K. Is originality more important to you than telling a story or creating characters?*
>
> *D.M. What's important is a really simple question 'Is it good? Is it good or not?' And, if you are true to yourself originality happens by default because every single person in the world has as an original personality as an iris. It seems that it is not original and that we are like other people and that one book is just like another book if we allow our true selves to be overly doctored or influenced by 'the other' or 'the others' but if you mine yourself deep enough then the metals you will find will be precious and original so originality is not a thing but an absence of other things.*[19]

These three people: my friend, Sargy Mann, the psycho-analyst, Marion Milner and the novelist, David Mitchell, all of them in their own unique individual manner, produced from their own core creator soul.

There are two principles that come together in each of these persons. The first is that what differentiates something that is living from something that is inorganic is that in the latter all activity occurs through the impact upon it of an object that is no part of itself. It only moves if it is moved. A living thing though has a source of action entirely from within it. This is so of all living things but with the human animal there is present a principle that is lacking in animals that are not human. This principle is awareness. Awareness is an inner mirror that tells me what I am doing. This can perhaps be best illustrated by differentiating between the experience when a monkey looks at a mirror and when a primate, be it a gorilla or a chimpanzee, does the same. Prior to producing the mirror a blob of red paint is dabbed onto the animal's face. When the monkey looks at the mirror it scratches at the image on the mirror; when a primate sees on the mirror the red spot on its face it scratches not the mirror but its own face. (This is why it is justly said by those, like Jane Goodall for instance, that the primates of all other human animals are clearly closest to humans in that there is in them that elemental sharing of the 'inner mirror.') So this is the first principle: that there is awareness of action in the human being so we move now to the second principle.

Although there are seven billion people on the planet there are no two human beings who look exactly the same. And the source of action in one is not the same as in another. There are no two sources of action which are exactly the same. The inner mirror reflects the action which is different in one than in another. Sargy Mann is getting at this when he says:

> *I think that one reason why great figurative painters are different, why a Titian is not like a Piero della Francesca or, a Matisse is not like Cézanne, is because each artist has had to find his own way of harnessing his skills and his temperament, his feelings and his intellect.*[20]

Sargy expresses it by saying that each artist has to find his own way of harnessing his skills, temperament, feelings and intellect. I don't think *skills*, *feelings* and *intellect* capture it though the word *temperament* comes closer to it. Even *temperament* is not right because *temperament* is a state of mind produced from an undefinable source. The words that give best expression to that source are in this genre: *essence*, *soul*, *lifeblood*. So just as no two people are physically exactly the same so also the essence, soul or lifeblood are not the same.

So the first principle is a generalization that is applicable to all human beings whereas the second is personal and so has its focus upon the difference between what one human produces and another. The two principles interpenetrate. The generalized principle is correct and the second principle allows, as it were, the generalization to have seven billion sensibilities.

Notes

1. Freud, S. (1923). *The Ego and the Id*. S.E. v. XIX. p. 40. London: The Hogarth Press & The Institute of Psycho-Analysis.
2. Chesterton, G.K. *Robert Louis Stevenson*. p. 234. London: Hodder & Stoughton.
3. Berlin, Isaiah (1979). *Against the Current*. [The Counter-Enlightenment]. p. 8. London: The Hogarth Press.
4. Macmurray, John (1949). *Conditions of Freedom*. p. 2. Toronto: The Ryerson Press.
5. Collingwood, R.G. (1965/1938). *The Principles of Art*. pp. 112–113. Oxford: Clarendon Press.
6. Freud, S. (1920). *Beyond the Pleasure Principle*. S.E.v. XVIII. pp. 27–28. London: The Hogarth Press & The Institute of Psycho-Analysis.

7. Hobson, Peter (2002). *The Cradle of Thought.* pp. 178–179. London: Palgrave Macmillan.
8. Milner, Marion (1987). *The Suppressed Madness of Sane Men.* p. 3. London & New York: Tavistock Publications.
9. Toynbee, Arnold, J. (1969). *Experiences.* p. 163. London: Oxford University Press.
10. Ibid., p. 163.
11. Thompson, Francis (1913). *The Works of Francis Thompson – Vol. III – Prose.* p. 162. London: Burns & Oates.
12. '[M]y mother mentioned that at the age of four, I was balancing on the back fence, arms outstretched, calling myself an "eppy plane." ' Bird, Nancy (1990). *My God! It's a Woman.* p. 9. Sydney: Angus and Robertson.
13. Mann, Peter and Sargy Mann (2008). *Sargy Mann.* p. 68. SP Books.
14. Mann, Sargy (2016). *Perceptual Systems, an Inexhaustible Reservoir of Information and the Importance of Art.* SP books.
15. Ibid., pp. 26–27.
16. Ibid., p. 28.
17. Ibid., pp. 28–29.
18. Milner, Marion (1987). *The Suppressed Madness of Sane Men.* p. 230 [*The Ordering of Chaos*]. London & New York: Tavistock Publications.
19. David Mitchell interviewed at the New Zealand Writers' Festival. Recorded on the Book Show on 21st January 2009.
20. Mann, Peter and Sargy Mann (2008). *Sargy Mann.* p. 68. SP Books.

Chapter 2

The unformed ego

> *It is the hardest thing in the world to shake off superstitious prejudices: they are sucked in as it were with our mother's milk; and growing up with us at a time when they take the fastest hold and make the most lasting impressions, become so interwoven into our very constitutions, that the strongest good sense is required to disengage ourselves from them.*[1]
> —Gilbert White [The Natural History of Selborne]

A man once came into my consulting-room and said 'I have never been formed.' It stands out in my mind because this is the situation with many people but this is the only occasion I came across in which the person was *aware* that he had not been formed. So this man was an exception. Because this man was aware of his inner state it signified that it was in the process of formation. When there is an image of a dysfunctional state of mind it means that it is already embraced within the personality and thus in a state of progress towards formation.

Once the state has been inwardly pictured; it is no longer in wild disarray but enveloped within an image. When something is dreamt it is already undergoing creation. This is based on the idea that something dreamt or pictured within the imagination means also that this pictorial image is the product of something being formed. Bion formulated this by saying that a *beta element* is transformed through *alpha function* and the consequence is the production of a dream and he meant by this not only a dream we have at night but what he referred to as a waking-dream or in any wayward thought or product of the imagination. Such an inner vision is the product of a creative happening. Psychic images not only portray life events but also form them and bring things into existence that were not there before. This transformed event now contained within a picture so the wild beasts roaming on the prairie are brought into a fenced-in enclosure and slowly tamed. In the National Gallery in London there is a painting by Turner of a ship in a storm. If I were on that ship in the storm I would be falling over, thrown this way and that, gripping hold of the rail round the deck, desperately trying to avoid falling into the sea. When I am looking at Turner's painting my feet are planted firmly on the ground; I am not being thrown hither and thither; the boat and the storm are now appropriated into the painting. If I construct an inner image of this sort, it embraces and transforms the wild anarchy. So the word 'image' is inadequate; it has a functional goal which is to embrace and penetrate the inner undigested elements. Image does not convey the function of gathering the elements into a coherent assembly. So I will use the musical term *composer*.

The surmise here refers to the core of the personality but in the next chapter the functions that are subsidiary to the central core will be reviewed. Some of these subsidiary functions are well developed and others are poorly formed. It seems that the reason why some are poorly formed is because the core ego is itself not satisfactorily formed. In other words there may be some malformation in this centre, the consequences of which only become clearly visible when one of the subsidiary functions is working at a poor standard. In other words malformation in the nucleus of the personality is inferred from the fact that a function flowing from it is not fully developed. That a particular function may be malfunctioning is sometimes felt as despair, despondency or a sense of hopelessness.

I will give a personal example of this state of mind. On a certain occasion I was in a distressed state. My mind was in turbulence. I was in a wild chaotic state. My ship was in a storm. I could see no solution. I was at a dead end. Fortuitously a friend asked me to accompany him to a cottage that sat on the saddle of a hill, on each side of which were beautiful views. It was not my own country and English was not my friend's first language. Apart from myself there came my friend's brother and two old associates of his. I stayed for five days at this cottage and the routine of the day was like this. We all rose in the morning at about seven and we were each served with a cup of tea. Then we went for a walk that lasted about half an hour and then returned to breakfast. When this was over my friend, his brother and two associates sat down at a table and played cards. I had with me a history of the country and a couple of other books and, armed with them, I went into the garden and sat and read until lunchtime. It was reflective reading. I was in no hurry and I quite often stopped and allowed random thoughts to stray across my mind. After lunch I had a rest and in the late afternoon my friend, his brother and the other two people and myself went for a drive through a countryside that was new to me. In the evening we had dinner. One of the party had brought a bottle of whisky and he gave to each one of us a night-cap and after a few relaxed exchanges of conversation we all went to bed. That was the routine and each of the five days was similar.

* * *

We can ask the question why it is that a shared experience can be taken in. It is because psychotic is equivalent to alone and isolated. Psychosis *is* isolation and it is a principle that only a shared reality can be taken in; this is because when something is able to be taken in it is because it has been created and creation occurs through the joining of two persons. A baby comes into being because a sperm and an ovum have interpenetrated. This is the case with a physical baby but the same principle applies with the arrival of a new thought, a new idea, a new image.

These emerge through the soul-to-soul connection between two different persons but who share a communicative milieu. So it is a belief that only a shared reality can be taken in. In popular discourse beliefs are confined to the sphere of religion but they also rule with great power in the field of science but, because beliefs are so evident in the sphere of religion, let us have a brief look at how they operate there. In certain Christian denominations it is believed that Jesus was born of a virgin; that his mother was not penetrated and inseminated through a man's penis entering her vagina and expelling semen to fertilize an egg which then implants on the wall of her womb. The Christian belief that this did not happen to Mary, the mother of Jesus, is visualized in art with an angel confronting Mary and delivering a message, a seed, from God into her womb. Many artists, like Leonard da Vinci, Crivelli or Fra Angelico, have painted this scene with their own characteristic imagery. Yet we all know that a foetus does not emerge into the woman's womb unless an egg has previously been fertilized by the semen emitted from the man's penis. This belief is an attempt to explain genius by attributing to God, a transcendent being, the responsibility for what seems to be a more-than-human endowment. How is it that the world has been blessed on occasions with people like Socrates, the Buddha, the prophet Isaiah, Jesus, Joan of Arc, Muhammad, Raphael, Moses Maimonides, Michelangelo, Kant, Shakespeare, Newton, Darwin, Einstein to mention just some of the most prominent and famous? Genius has been described as someone endowed with a divine spark; the idea that God, a being from the heavens, has fertilized the minds of these great people. So a belief is a way of explaining a supreme human quality and even the power of evil men like Hitler, Stalin, Mao-Tse-Tung or Robert Mugabe is attributed to a diabolic charism. Jesus was betrayed by Judas, one of his chosen twelve apostles and Saint Luke in the gospel which he wrote said that the devil entered into the heart of Judas.[2] In other words an extreme power, good or evil, is attributed to an agency beyond and above the normal human processes of achievement. Someone with charism is able to 'draw people in.' This is because the person's identity is that of a child; a child has that capacity to draw people's affection, love and adoration, even.

I have said that such beliefs govern not only religious people and communities but also scientific research. All beliefs, religious, scientific and artistic, come from God. What an outrageous statement. Let me explain. We do not conceptualize the world as it is but how an authority has declared it to be. So the priestly author in a particular section of the Book of Genesis told us that the world was fashioned by God in seven days; well six days because on the seventh God rested as he certainly deserved to do. But each day, according to commentators, refers to a long period of time and those who have calculated the age of the Earth according to the Book of Genesis put it at about 6,004 years. Of course we all know that the Earth is about 4.5 billion years old. The point I am making is that we (or perhaps I should say I) do not know the age of the Earth. My belief that it is 4.5 billion years old is based on what has been passed to me by astronomers and geologists and I believe what they have told me just as people in the past believed what the author of Genesis told them. My knowledge of the world is based on belief. If

I had lived in the fifteenth century I would have known that the Earth is the centre of the solar system. Then God intervened in human history. This time God was called Copernicus and he declared in 1540 that the sun was the centre of the solar system and that our planet travelled around it in perfect circles. So, living just after Copernicus, I knew that the Sun was at the centre and our Earth travelled around it in perfect circles but my grandson, who was born in 1620, told me I was quite wrong because an astronomer, called Johannes Kepler, had shown in the year 1609 that the Earth and all the planets travelled around the Sun in elliptical orbits. So Copernicus was God for 69 years until he was dethroned by Kepler. I now believe not according to Copernicus but according to Kepler. In a similar way the God Newton declared in 1687 the principle of gravitation and I believed this because the Newton God had declared it. Then a new God arose called Einstein who in 1915 published his work on relativity in which he refuted Newton and the God called Einstein, in whom we now believe, knows that gravity is not a force but a distortion of the time-space dimension.

What I am getting at is that we do not know the world as it is but we see it according to the proclamations of certain Gods. Each new God corrects the beliefs of the previous one but a new God will always appear to challenge and displace the old one. Therefore we do not know the world as it is but we base ourselves on a series of beliefs originating in the proclamations of a series of Gods. The Gods I have referred to are those whose proclamations relate to the rhythms within the solar system and the regular movement of the solar system within the Milky Way galaxy and the trajectory of this our galaxy in relation to the myriad galaxies that make up our universe. We may refer to these Gods as serial monotheism because at any one period of time it is *one* God whose proclamations we believe and then when that God is displaced he is supplanted by another so we call it serial monotheism but we are about now to move in a different world which we name *the human condition*. The attachment to a belief is a sign that the ego is unformed and the more the ego is unformed the greater the belief system and the contemporary growth in terrorism is because there is an epidemic of unformed egos. We may want in the discussion to reflect on what in our modern culture has been responsible for bringing this about.

Our knowledge of the world of human beings is conditioned not by monotheism but by polytheism. There are many gods proclaiming the nature of the human world and they frequently contradict each other. I give you this quote from Mcneile Dixon:

> *Pleasure, said Epictetus, is the chief good. It is the chiefest of evils, said Antisthenes. Men, declared Rousseau, are naturally good; they are naturally bad, said Machiavelli. It is on the same evidence that distinguished people contradict each other. Virtue, proclaimed the Stoics, is sufficient for happiness. Without external goods it is not sufficient, said Aristotle.*[3]

So Epictetus, Antisthenes, Rousseau, Machiavelli, the Stoics and Aristotle were each Gods but Gods who contradicted each other. So the *distinguished people*, the Gods of Philosophy, differ profoundly from one another. And these Gods have also their believers, just as the Gods of the solar system have theirs. The difference is that, with few exceptions, all people believe what Kepler, Newton and Einstein proclaimed but as soon as we enter the portals of Philosophy there are many Gods with a whole range of believers. In the ancient world there was Socrates, Plato, Aristotle; in the mediaeval world there was Moses Maimonides, Thomas Aquinas, Averroes; in the modern era Rousseau, Descartes, Kant. It is definitely polytheism: many Gods, each with their cohort of believers and those that believe in one of these Gods are often in violent opposition to the proclamations of a different God, a God whose proclamations are antagonistic to my God in whom I believe.

This diversity is also so within any one discipline of thought, whether it be History, Anthropology, Economics, Sociology or Psychology. So also within psychoanalysis Freud has his believers, Jung has his believers, Melanie Klein has her believers, Fairbairn has his believers, Heinz Kohut has his believers, Winnicott has his believers, Bion has his believers and each group of these believers follow *their* God and repudiate other Gods. The point of similarity between these philosophical or psychological Gods and those of the solar system is that in neither is the reality itself apprehended but rather what is proclaimed by the God to whom I have bowed my head in humble submission. It is the alarming truth that we do not see the human environment as it is. What about these Gods like Freud, Jung or Melanie Klein; did they see the human world as it is? Each one glimpsed truly one aspect of the human condition. Frequently they then generalized this and made the glimpse of one particularity into a nostrum for a much wider spectrum of the human world. Also this glimpse was a momentary vision seen through the lens of one individual. And we all attach ourselves to the vision of one of these Gods. Why? Bion said that there is a hatred of learning from experience:

There is a hatred of having to learn from experience at all, and lack of faith in the worth of such kind of learning.[4]

But wherefore this hatred and lack of faith in such learning? Why is it so? It is because it faces us with our unformation or even deformation. I wonder if we can get some purchase on this by considering the case of Kepler. He tracked the orbit of Mars and, contrary to the general belief in the God Copernicus, he discovered that Mars's orbit around the sun was not circular but elliptical but it took him six years before he dared to declare it. Why? I think it is that we are all desirous of being in a troupe, a company. To be entirely on my own, out of kilter with the rest of my fellows, is alarming, frightening. And yet it seems that one's own experience is unique. One person's experience is never an exact simulacrum of that of another. There is uniqueness and sharedness for every human being. We are each of us part of a reality in which we share and, at the same time, each is unique. But there is something about getting in touch with this uniqueness that is hated. Experience is this getting in touch with what is unique. Sexual orgasm is one of the supreme delights for a human being and it is, in its essential nature, the union between two people. Aloneness is orgasm's opposite and it is hated.

There is a difference between being alone and being isolated. What is it? When I am alone I am in a shared world; the features of my face as different from that of any other compatriot and yet I share with others a forehead, two eyes, two ears, a nose and a chin. I share yet I am different. The individual who is isolated is cut adrift from the shared world of which he or she is a part.

Just as my physiognomy is never quite the same as that of another so also this is so of my mental orientation. There is something shared with another and yet there is a difference. To be wholly at-one with another in everything is a denial of who I am. This is to introduce the relationship between someone and a God whom he believes in, the God being Melanie Klein or Tolstoy or Bergson. Just as my physiognomy is the same but different so also I cannot be Melanie Klein, or Winnicott or Bion. If I were then I would not have my own selfhood. I have to differ in some respects.

* * *

Two further aspects to this need consideration: that the person here today is not the same as the person who was here yesterday. Development or deterioration is always in process. Now this is so of the individual but it is also so of social groups. In Britain in the 1950s homosexual acts between men were a criminal offence and termed 'acts of gross indecency.' Fifty years later a sexual partnership between two men has the blessing of society and is referred to as *gay marriage*. This symptomatic change has its roots in a deep transformation of the social group. The social group is different in its orientation. Other symptom changes within the same society and within the same time period are the abolition of the death penalty, the increase in divorce and its being viewed in greater favour, the condemnation of fox hunting and the great increase in restaurants serving food from Thailand, Korea and India. So this state of mind that is being recommended can, under favourable circumstances, discover the deep currents that have given rise to these surface differences. Social groups are in a state of change and development constantly. There have been periods when a society has continued for centuries in one mode such as the Dark Ages in southern Europe or the Mandarin governance in China. There have also been times of rapid revolution and change that have taken place within twenty or thirty years.

* * *

I take you back to this time when I spent five days at this cottage on the hill. The drive from the city to this cottage took about three hours and I sat in the back of the car with my friend who had invited me and we talked. I also talked with him on each of the five days when on our morning walk before breakfast and also during the evening drive. The conversation with my friend was relaxed but personal. There was nothing theoretical or general about the way he talked with me. He shared with me some quite intimate failings of his, particularly events which had occurred when he was a young man. He was now in his late seventies. This honest intercourse that passed between us had a fertilizing effect. It is also that a personal sharing of this intimate and creative kind occurs when there is a giving from the other. Rousseau said, and I believe correctly:

it is a bad way of reading another man's heart to conceal one's own.[5]

On about the third day when I was sitting in the garden reading a very definite image came into my mind and I understood that having the image indicated that rather than being ruled by the storm that was raging inside me it was now a personal creation within me. The composer had been at work and produced the image that both embraced and transformed the inner commotion. So some unformed function of my personality was beginning to be formed. The sign that this was so was the very definite image that traced its being across my inner radar and the despondent state was dissipating. The composer had been productive. Turner had now fashioned a painting of the inner storm and my feet stood on solid ground.

One reason why the *composer* functioned with a certain strength was that the person who had invited me to this cottage of his respected and encouraged my freedom. In those mornings when I used to sit in a chair out on the saddle of the hill and he was playing cards with his three friends there was never the slightest hint even that I should be joining with him and his friends. He entirely respected me and my activity and I think this contributed to the ability of the *composer* to do his work within me.

The point I want to stress is that there is a background assumption in nearly all psycho-analytic thinking. What is it? It is that we are all in possession of a fully formed ego. This leads an analyst to say to a patient that he or she is denying the pain (of something) or failing to remember, or failing to sympathize with someone in distress or failing to reflect upon an experience but this mode of communicating is based on the assumption that there is a fully formed ego which is able to bear pain, able to sympathize with another or able to remember or reflect on experience but is choosing not to do so. It leads also to analysts accusing themselves of not being able to manage certain emotional disturbances occurring in their patients. But it is not the preserve of patients alone who have unformed egos but rather it is so of everyone whatever their official role in life is. We are all only partly formed creatures. It is rare to encounter someone who has a fully formed ego. The analytic belief that we all have a fully formed ego greatly distorts our understanding of the human condition, the underlying understanding of most of our motivations.

I use the artist transforming wild nature into peaceful harmony as an analogy for the artist that is at work in the personality. I have been using the term *composer* but artist could also be used. This is the inner craftsman that operates in the core of the personality. This artist is the inner *creative principle*, the creator which is synonymous with Bion's *alpha function*. What I want to emphasize here is that this artist within does not just transform inner storms, inner anxiety, inner pain but creates the *me* that is. Me is not me in the absence of this inner transformer. The *I*, the *Me*, is a creation. I give you this quote which is from David Shulman's book on Sanskrit thinking in mediaeval India:

> *our ability to identify anything at all, or to remember anything – even who we are – is entirely a matter of* bhavana, *a creative capacity situated at the core of the mind (*atma-guna*). We might think we are remembering objective experiences that are part of our cumulative repertoire of self-knowledge – but in fact we are re-creating them, or reimagining them.* Bhavana *brings the initial sensory mark or impression back to the surface, thus allowing for an immediate, nondubious perception.*[6]

Now those readers, who are good Freudian psycho-analysts, may want to reject this defining feature of the personality – because this view holds that *bhavana* is situated at the core of the mind (*atma-guna*) but this contradicts Freud's view that *Das Es*, the Id, is the mind's essential substance. For Freud says:

> *the ego is especially under the influence of perception, and that, speaking broadly, perceptions may be said to have the same significance for the ego as instincts have for the id. At the same time the ego is subject to the influence of the instincts, too, like the id, of which it is, as we know, only a specially modified part.*[7]

The ego here is not *atma-guna*, the core of the mind, but something that is subservient to the impact of inner and outer sensations. The instincts in Freud's account are not creators but machine like impulses. Freud used the word *triebe* which is usually translated as *drives*. The crucial point is when he states that the ego is only a specially modified part of the id; in other words just part of a machine-like impulse. He thus makes the id the foundation stone of the personality. This is the opposite to the view of these Sanskrit thinkers in Mediaeval South India. Those reading these contradictory views need to make a decision as to which of them corresponds most clearly to his or her experience. These two views, the Sanskrit one and Freud's, are in opposition to each other and either one or the other has to be chosen and established. It leads to muddled thinking if both are accepted without reconciling the contradiction.

Now it may sound as though this is abstract theorizing of no importance but the way we think about this can throw light on disturbances of thought in psychotic patients. Sometimes it is that what is inner and what is outer are not differentiated. An hallucination is an example of someone thinking an inner event is an outer one. There is also the phenomenon of negative hallucination where a visible object in the outer world is obliterated. I have in my consulting-room a statuette made of Copenhagen China of a woman with a baby on her lap. It sits on a table and is about eighteen inches in length and a foot high. A man, Antonio, sitting in a chair facing this statue at about the distance of four feet, suddenly said one day 'Oh look you've got a new statue.' He had been coming five days a week for three years and the piece of sculpture had been there the whole of that time. He had been in the grip of a negative hallucination for those three years. I think it likely that the negative hallucination is primary and the positive hallucination is superimposed on the negative one. The world we perceive is a creation but what is it that determines whether it is the creation of what is or the fashioning of a false conjecture? It may seem odd to hear me talking of the creation of what is already there. If it is there it does not need to be created; surely creation is of what is not there? The creative act endows what is there with new life, a new soul. An event has occurred in my life and unexpectedly it has an energy that it had not had before. A wooden Pinocchio has become a living person.

The kernel of the matter is this. I have said that the core of the mind is a creator, a composer, an artist and yet, if we follow our Sanskrit metaphysicians there is a more fundamental principle that produces the composer. The *I* and the *Me* has its origin not in itself but in the fantastic fact of existence of which I am a part, an exemplar. The recognition of this leads to creation of reality which is faithful to what is, but non-recognition of it leads to the fashioning of illusion. I am not the author of existence but rather I am lived by existence. Why did Picasso become a painter? Why did Plato become a philosopher? Why did Alan Turing become an inventor? They did not know and we do not know. They were lived by destiny.

* * *

I referred to Picasso, Plato and Turing and asked the question about the source of their creative leaps that brought such illuminating insights into the world. In the next chapter there is a long disquisition which is an attempt to answer that question. In a brief summary it is when the individual who is transient realizes himself as part of the universe that is infinite and eternal. He is part of something greater. It is his participation in this which shines forth in the lives of people of such magnitude – those geniuses who have changed the way we know the world.

To come back to Antonio who saw my statuette for the first time. The core of the personality had been disabled for three years. What this means is that authority or the 'generalized other' smothers and dominates this inner core. There is another way of thinking about this. It is, as I have opined, that everything that is 'seen' or 'perceived,' is a creation and so Antonio could not see my Copenhagen statuette because his creative core was disabled. So he was not in the room with another person whom he perceived through his own perceptual functions but is under the impact of an 'authority voice' which says, 'You are now in a room with a psycho-analyst' so he speaks accordingly in a depersonalized tone as if he were a newscaster on the radio reading out a text which he had been given. There is no connection, fashioned by his inner core, between him and this person who is in the consulting-room with him. His inner creative core is strangled by this paralyzing force like a fly caught in a spider's web and wrapped around so that it cannot move or change position. The crucial statement is that there is no connection between him and another person. What replaces this is an institution called 'psycho-analysis' in conjunction with another institution called an 'analysand' or a 'patient.' But it is not this particular analysand or this particular patient but a class or a category called analysand or patient. What is present is the conjunction of two amorphous lumps of reality. That moment when he sees the statuette on my table coincides with a sudden opening of him to a person, a person who happens to have this particular statuette on his table. No other psycho-analyst has this particular statuette on his consulting-room. So he sees that this particular person, Neville, is present and in conversation with him but also at that moment he is no longer a unit in the amorphous category called 'patient.' Suddenly he is Antonio – yes this person Antonio and there is no other Antonio than him. So now there is no longer psycho-analysis and patient jangling together but Antonio and Neville in communication with each other.

What has been said here has been given insightful understanding by R.G. Collingwood. He is talking of the artistry of poets but what he says about poets applies also to the 'poetry of psycho-analytic practice.' What Collingwood says about poets applies also to the language as expressed by psycho-analysts in their consulting-rooms. I have quoted what he says in the last chapter where he emphasizes that description generalizes and therefore the particular individual insight or feeling is put into a filing cabinet under a particular categorized title.

So Collingwood differentiates 'description' from 'expression.' Description refers to a psycho-analyst and a patient whereas 'expression' refers to Neville communicating with Antonio. He is saying that the kind of psychological vocabulary which is general rather than peculiar damages poetical uniqueness. This 'psychological vocabulary' that damages poetical individuality also destroys the particular individual intercourse occurring between Neville and Antonio. So it is psycho-analytic theories which the clinician, in poet's mode, needs not to use. Many analysts do precisely what Collingwood says should not be done. How many times is someone described as being depressed? or projecting? or in the grip of projective identification? or denying? or borderline? or narcissistic? or psychotic? or neurotic? or schizophrenic? or bi-polar? Whenever this is done the personhood of the individual vanishes and a generalized nonentity takes occupation. As the Greek philosopher, Stilpo, says: *Those who speak of men in general; speak of nobody.*[8]

What needs examining however is why this 'authority' had such an invasive power in this man's inner world. In Sanskrit thinking *bhavana*, at the core of the personality, is responsible not just for informing me who I am but for fashioning that duality: inner/outer so this begins to throw some light on this patient. Is it that there is something wrong, something disabled, in the core of his personality? And that this disability prevents him from separating accurately what is inner from what is outer – this does not give an answer towards the resolution of his problem but it begins to place it in the right arena. If his core self is in some way maimed then I, as clinician, have to begin thinking 'What can I do, or what do I need to do' to start the work of rehabilitating his core self. When speaking thus it reminds me of the way a colleague's patient needed 'Pure You.' It was important to her that she could engage with the inner soul of her analyst without any of her analytic theories. It was the 'Pure You' of her analyst that enabled her to begin the work of making, of fashioning, of creating her own core self. The 'Pure You' reminds me of the person who told me of some new zoological research where the DNA was extracted from the male semen but this semen did nevertheless fertilize the female ovum. She needed 'Pure Neville' without any of his cherished theories. I think Bion was onto the same issue when he talked of being without Memory or Desire. This is also expressed in the Sanskrit work on the imagination:

> *closer to our primary theme is the relatively unfocused, even floating, receptive attentiveness, neither inward- nor outward-directed, perhaps analogous on one level to the default awareness of a south Indian deity. Such states are conducive to sudden moments of unpredictable insight or 'realization.'*[9]

It has also been stated in different language by Marion Milner. She says:

> *I myself had learnt when writing the Joanna Field books, for instance, about having observed that there were two kinds of attention, both necessary, a wide unfocused stare, and a narrow focused penetrating kind, and that the wide kind brought remarkable changes in perception and enrichment of feeling.*[10]

When she refers here to a wide unfocussed stare this is another way of referring to 'without memory or desire' or Shulman's description of unfocussed floating receptive attentiveness. General Smuts says the same thing when talking of the need to arrive at principles governing a large range of facts:

> *The road is to be discovered, not so much by minute local inspection as by wide roaming and exploration and surveying over large districts.*[11]

I may be getting away from the central point: that there is a creative core that fashions even me, who I am. The patient who is in silence may, I believe, be communicating in a deep way with the analyst, therapist or . . . the receptive other. I have had a couple of patients who have communicated with me in this mode and, for each, it has been important not to know external biographical facts about me because they interfere with this primary knowing. These biographical facts about the patient also interfere with the analyst's knowing of his or her patient. There is a level of sensitive affinity which is the prime organ of communication and this is, in essence, independent of the 'outer clothing' be it that both are educated in a psycho-analytic frame of thinking or that both are Jewish, or both are English or both are young, or both are old, or both are women, or both are men. One may be a prostitute in Madrid, the other a ski instructor in Norway, another a taxi driver in New York, another a Trappist monk, another an investigative journalist. The communicative level is quite independent of these outer markers. The silent patient is often tuned into this 'state of mind' level.

I had a patient once, coming five times a week, who was totally silent for three months but there was powerful communication going on during this time and productive work was done and this also happened on subsequent occasions and it became clear that an important emotional work was being done, much deeper work than when there was verbal intercourse between us.

Notes

1 White, Gilbert (1788/1978). *The Natural History of Selborne*. p. 184. Penguin Books.
2 Luke Chapter 22 verse 3.
3 Mcneile Dixon, W. (1958). *The Human Situation*. pp. 53–54. Penguin Books.
4 Bion, W.R. (1961/1968). *Experiences in Groups*. p. 89. London: Tavistock Publications.
5 Rousseau, Jean-Jacques (1973). *The Confessions*. [Book Two 1728–1731]. p. 83. Penguin Books.
6 Shulman, David (2012). *More Than Real: A History of the Imagination in South India*. p. 164. Cambridge, MA & London: Harvard University Press.
7 Freud, S. (1923). *The Ego and the Id*. S.E. v. XIX. p. 40. London: The Hogarth Press & The Institute of Psycho-Analysis.
8 Mcneile Dixon, W. (1958). *The Human Situation*. p. 175. Penguin Books.
9 Shulman, David (2012). *More Than Real: A History of the Imagination in South India*. p. 141. Cambridge, MA & London: Harvard University Press.
10 Milner, Marion (1987). *The Suppressed Madness of Sane Men*. p. 81. [*1952* – The Framed Gap]. London & New York: Tavistock Publications.
11 Smuts, Jan Christiaan (1926/1996). *Holism and Evolution*. p. 7. Gestalt Journal Press Inc. (A division of The Center of Gestalt Development – PO Box 990, Highland, New York 12528. ISBN # 0-939266-26-)

Chapter 3

Foundation for growth of mind

In the last chapter I said that the ego is never, or only very rarely, fully formed. I was referring especially to the core of the personality. In the second chapter I put the view that the ego is a creator in its essential nature; the ego is not composed of a series of joined-up instincts which happen also to be creative but that it is an independent autonomous creator in its own right. In the last chapter I linked this up with the nature of life, of living things. The analyst who emphasized this was Elliot Jaques who thought that even so primitive a creature as an amoeba, a single-celled organism, exercised choice so that if faced with two pieces of food it chose which of the two it wanted to ingest.

There are many functions in the personality that flow out from this central creator. I want now to name, not all of them, but some of them:

Functions in relation to the Self	*Functions in relation to the Other*
Capacity to imagine	Capacity to intuit
Capacity to feel	Capacity to relate
Capacity to abstract & think	Capacity to like
Capacity to remember	Capacity to sympathize
Capacity to relax	Capacity to connect sexually
Capacity for tacit knowledge	
Capacity to take in	
Capacity to take in and retain it within	
Capacity to establish good experiences within	
Capacity to suffer painful happenings	
Capacity to unify and create coherence	
Capacity to know that I am a living being	

Functions of the personality

There are many functions in the personality. Some of them are so basic that it is difficult to realize that a function may either be absent or very undeveloped or partially undeveloped. Some examples:

Example 1: A psychiatrist was treating a man who believed that he was responsible for 9/11. She, the psychiatrist, could very easily see that it was a delusion that he was responsible for 9/11 but there was a more basic one which she, the psychiatrist, could not see, and had difficulty in believing. It was that the man did not know he was alive. I said to the psychiatrist that there were two things: one the fact of being alive and the other the knowledge of being alive. This man did not **know** he was alive. She found it hard to grasp this and yet there is a link between the delusion that he was responsible for 9/11 and not knowing that he was alive. It is a safe principle that a sign that a function in the personality is poorly developed is the presence of a harsh super-ego. So this man lacks a very fundamental function: the knowledge that he is alive. To know that I am alive I need my inner productive imagination to create the aliveness; otherwise I am a walking robot. The personality has been assaulted by alarming happenings and these reside in the personality as foreign objects that drive the individual this way or that way. Bion referred to these as *beta elements* but in order to become occurrences which the person has embraced and made part of himself they need to come under the direction of what Bion called *alpha function* and which I refer to in this book as the creator which is the core of the personality. In Bion's language they become *alpha elements* when they have been processed by *alpha function*. In my language they become personal qualities or character traits.

In an autobiographical book of mine entitled *A Different Path*[1] I speak of a crisis in my early life. It was when I left the Church of which I had been a priest and therefore an active member. My father was distressed when this happened. I knew he was distressed but his unhappiness was not alive to me. Why? It was masked by my own egotistical concerns. Today, fifty years later, my father's disappointment is alive. I feel for him in a way which I did not at the time. This means that my own sensibility was severely impoverished at the time. I was on a determined goal-directed path. The goal was the accomplishment of my own sensuous pleasure. But why is it different now? What has changed? I will put forth my thesis.

There was a belief underlying all my thinking but also underlying the thinking of nearly all philosophical and psychological descriptions concerning the human condition. In the introduction to the Gifford Lectures John Macmurray says this:

> *The general subject of these lectures was dictated by a double criticism of our philosophical tradition. The traditional point of view is both theoretical and egocentric. It is theoretical in that it proceeds as though the Self were a pure subject for whom the world is object. This means that the point of view adopted by our philosophy is that of the Self in its moment of reflection, when its activity is directed towards the acquirement of knowledge. Since the Self in reflection is withdrawn from action, withdrawn into itself, withdrawn from participation in the life of the world into contemplation, this point of view is egocentric. The Self in reflection is self-isolated from the world which it knows. This theoretical and egocentric character of our philosophy is not doctrinal. It is a presupposition, generally unconscious, implicit in philosophical procedures.*[2]

The crucial words here are *withdrawn from participation in the life of the world*. I was in a system of thinking whose central belief was that the *I* was isolated from the *life of the world* and this meant all those around me: my mother, my father, my brother, my sister and the many friends that surrounded me. I was in isolation and each of these people of the world were outside of me. Therefore there was an egotism that was backed up and supported by a belief system that was egocentric. The *I* was installed in an egocentric neighbourhood. And so the focus of attention was on the *I*, the *me* so my father's distress was not the focus of concern. This implies that only one object can be attended to by the mind in any one slice of time. So now the question is this: why is it that my father's distress is alive to me now today? It has to be that I, the *I*, is no longer isolated. The *I* and the *Other* are in a shared medium and that it is this partnership and not *I* or the *Other* that is the subject both of action and the registration of action. So my father's distress is not now the distress of an *Other* but a distress that is his and mine because we are in a shared domain. There is an underlying sense of this field of action in which both participate because father and son are related to one another and a relation can only occur if there is a something that is shared by both.

* * *

Now to come back to the psychiatrist who was treating the man who had that delusion that he was responsible for 9/11 and, as just said, this particular instance can be surmised from the presence of a harsh super-ego: 'it is you, you wicked man, who are responsible for 9/11.' The clinical task however is to arrive at the 'hidden delusion' – i.e. the belief that he is not alive. Now one might ask the question: 'Why is it that the knowledge of the absence cannot be accepted, taken as a scientific fact?' I think the answer lies in shame. We are all developing; all living things develop and there is a built in knowledge of both the goal towards which we are heading and our actual state at present. Someone born with six fingers, as in the case of Ann Boleyn, is ashamed. Ann Boleyn was careful to hide the hand which had six fingers. So there is a knowledge of how the mind-body set-up should be, as opposed to how it actually is. Shame indicates that the actual set-up is disfigured. We are humans but the animal in us plays a big part in our mental life. In the animal kingdom the defective one is torn to death. The damaged bird is pecked to death by its fellows in the flock. So there is the built-in opposition to that which is deformed in us but this refers not only to a misshapen body but also to mental and emotional deformity. So rather than accept the fact that knowledge of aliveness is unformed this man has a tyrant that condemns him as wicked. It was Lord Melbourne who said:

> *It wounds a man less to confess that he has failed in any pursuit through idleness, neglect, the love of pleasure, etc., etc., which are his own faults, than through incapacity and unfitness, which are the fault of his nature.*[3]

And so, being ashamed, he does not come to the view that he is lacking in the knowledge of his aliveness, or aware of the fact, but instead is overwhelmed by a savage condemnation. 'You see you are a wicked fellow – you destroyed the Twin Towers.' It is, as just instanced, that we are all inheritors of the evolutionary principle whereby the damaged or ill-formed organism is destroyed in favour of the healthy organism. I am invoking here Darwin's principle of selection. But this man is not aware of this punishing despot but of his wicked act – destroying the twin towers in New York. The evident omnipotence is present to cover up this inner deficiency. He can swagger around 'I, the great *I* destroyed the Twin Towers you know.' Our clinical task is therefore to locate the undeveloped function and throw light upon it. If we do detect it and reveal it to our patient the news is not happily received. We need to do it tactfully but even with tact we become the target of rage – the negative transference, the only true negative transference. There is often a focus within psycho-analysis upon the omnipotence rather than on the undeveloped function which it masks. So this is an example of someone whose knowledge that he was alive was undeveloped.

In this particular case how was it possible to arrive at the fact that the undeveloped function was knowledge that he was alive? It was that when the psychiatrist in a subsequent interview was exploring his attitude to the people killed in the 9/11 disaster. He said 'Of course I know about dying; I am dead myself.' This remark was a trigger that then brought the patient's dead mechanical tone of voice into focus for the therapist. She then came to realize that this was the patient's basic assumption.

Example 2: A therapist was treating a man who had had five previous therapists. The therapist started by believing that the man was passive-aggressive. Then he realized that whenever he spoke the man experienced his speech as a violent assault. This was even when he said mild things like 'Maybe, after having had several bad experiences with therapists you feel cautious about starting therapy with me' – or 'I sense you get frightened when your wife gets angry with you.' Whatever the therapist *said* was a violent assault. The therapist decided to stay silent. The patient also stayed silent and this continued for many, many sessions. After these silent sessions the therapist suddenly realized in a moment of illumination that any speech was an assault. So how was it that the silent sessions brought about a realization for him? We do not understand something through speech. Speech points to something more fundamental than speech. It is what Rousseau referred to as the *language of expression*:

> *By neglecting the language of expression we have lost the most forcible mode of speech. The spoken word is always weak, and we speak to the heart rather through the eyes then the ears. In our attempt to appeal to reason only, we have reduced our precepts to words, we have not embodied them in deed. Mere reason is not active; occasionally she restrains, more rarely she stimulates, but she never does any great thing. Small minds have a mania for reasoning. Strong souls speak a very different language, and it is by this language that men are persuaded and driven to action.*[4]

Michael Polanyi referred to this as *tacit knowledge*. In the moment of understanding there is a happening in our minds which is beyond the words. Speech without this understanding is terrifying. It is a thunderous noise assaulting us. So what was happening in those silent sessions? I think the capacity for understanding develops through the mother's reverie or contemplation of her baby. This state in the mother is not just receptive but generative which is why I like to call it contemplation which is an active mental gazing. But if someone has missed out on this as a baby, this neglect can be repaired in later life. I believe this was happening in those silent sessions. This function: the capacity for understanding was being created in the silence. An analyst presented some work of hers and, in discussion concerning these undeveloped functions she emphasized:

> *More specifically they* [the functions of the personality] *are evoked by the mother's qualities of mind, and the corollary – the absence of this state of mind has consequences. Mother's primary maternal preoccupation or riveted attention is the state of mind we are speaking about. The other quality of the maternal mind is its liveliness and responsiveness, the quality of going out to meet the other/baby, not just to contain it.*

The important point here is this meeting of the other, this encounter with the baby. This meeting is more important than the nurture of the baby. Ian Suttie emphasized the innate need for companionship which he placed as more central than the Freudian libido.

He says:

> *I saw the possibility that the biological need for nurture might be psychologically presented in the infant mind, not as a bundle of practical organic necessities and potential privations, but as a pleasure in responsive companionship and as a correlative discomfort in loneliness and isolation. The Freudian conception of self-expression as a 'detensioning' process or emotional evacuation now seemed to me to be false and in its place I imagined expression as an offering or stimulus directed to the other person, designed to elicit a response while love itself was essentially a state of active harmonious interplay. . . .*
>
> *. . . It differs fundamentally from psycho-analysis in introducing the conception of an innate need-for-companionship which is the infant's only way of self-preservation. This need, giving rise to parental and fellowship 'love,' I put in the place of the Freudian Libido, and regard it as genetically independent of genital appetite. The application of this conception seems to reorient the whole psycho-analytic dynamics.*[5]

The therapist, in those silent sessions, gave himself over to contemplation. If someone has missed out on this contemplation or reverie as a baby this neglect can be repaired in later life. I believe this was happening in those silent sessions. This function: the capacity for understanding was being created in the silence. The functions of the personality are evoked by the mother's qualities of mind, and the corollary – the absence of this state of mind has consequences. Mother's primary maternal preoccupation or riveted attention is the state of mind we are speaking about. The other quality of the maternal mind is its liveliness and responsiveness, the quality of going out to meet the other/baby, not just contain it. It is the inner attitude of mind that is generative. It is often said that the agent of change is in the interpretation in words delivered by the analyst. This is far too external a criterion. It is the inner movements of the mind that have an effect both on the analyst and the patient.

This 'going out to meet the baby' needs emphasis. There is a danger that 'contain' or 'reverie' might be distorted into a passive state. This is why I like to use the term *contemplation*. It is not passive but this phrase 'going out to meet the baby' (formulated by a colleague of mine) could, in no way, be twisted from active to passive. 'Contemplation' is more active than reverie – it carries the attitude of 'going out to meet the baby.' Peter Hobson says in his book *The Cradle of Thought*:

> *The person who is free to evaluate attachments is able to assimilate and <u>think about</u> her own past experiences in relationships, even when these have been unsatisfactory. She has mental space to relate to her own relations with others. She can reflect on her own feelings and impulses and can forgive and tolerate her own shortcomings. So, too, she has space to relate to her own baby as an independent and separate person and to be sensitive to her baby's states of mind in such a way that the baby is likely to become securely attached.*[6]

This is something which is well-known from the attachment literature but it is a remarkable finding: that the mother's own internal active reflective state is enabling for the child and, contrariwise, disabling if absent and it is not that the mother is saying to herself 'I must engage in reverie so my baby can find safety and security.' She does it naturally; it is a natural endowment. This is a different point of view from what Winnicott named *primary maternal preoccupation*, for this is something that is generated for a temporary period when the mother is pregnant and during the early weeks of the baby's life. This capacity that Hobson refers to here is something that is happening in the woman prior to pregnancy. It would be happening even if she never had a child. The important point made here by Peter Hobson is that even when the mother's experiences have been unsatisfactory it is her capacity to reflect on them that matters. When we take a history of a mother who has had many bad experiences, it does not tell us therefore that she will not be able to enliven her child because the crucial issue is whether she is able to think about her experiences, reflect upon them, let them pass unbidden across her inner radar screen. What is clear is that the active reflection transforms the experience from one that disables the personality to one that invigorates it.

When a history is taken it is essential that it is not interpreted that this event in the past has 'caused' the present distress because the main contributor is whether or not there is present a process of active transformation. The essence of being alive is that there is a creative principle at the root of the personality. It is what Bion referred to as *alpha function*. Without *alpha function* or what I refer to as the *creative core* the person is dead. Consider this poem by Thomas Hardy:

The Dead Man Walking

They hail me as one living,
    But don't they know
That I have died of late years,
    Untombed although?
I am but a shape that stands here,
    A pulseless mould,
A pale past picture, screening
    Ashes gone cold.
Not at a minute's warning,
    Not in a loud hour,
For me ceased Time's enchantments
    In hall and bower.
There was no tragic transit,
    No catch of breath,
When silent seasons inched me
    On to this death. . .
A Troubadour-youth I rambled
    With life for lyre,
The beats of being raging
    In me like fire
When I practised eyeing
    The goal of men
It iced me, and I perished
    A little then.
When passed my friend, my kinsfolk,
    Through the Last Door,
And left me standing bleakly,
    I died yet more;
And when my Love's heart kindled
    In hate of me,
Wherefore I knew not, died I
    One more degree.
And if when I died fully
    I cannot say,
And changed into the corpse-thing

>   I am to-day;
> Yet is it that, though whiling
>   The time somehow
> In walking, talking, smiling,
>   I live not now. (pp. 217–219, [Poem 166])

* * *

I mentioned that the *I* and the *Other* are in a shared medium. This is so important that it requires emphasis and elaboration. It is not just that *I* and the *Other* are passively inhabitants of the same environment but that the agent of action is neither the *I* nor the *Other* but the two, united together, are the subject of action. In sexual intercourse there is physical penetration and in the moment of orgasm an experience of joint togetherness. This moment of orgasm is a symbol for the shared medium in which the *I* and the *Other* are joined and become *one-in-action*. So the *I* as the source of action is the two, *I* and the *Other*, a joint actor. If the *I* is considered to be separate from the *Other* this is based on a false belief. Narcissism is the name given to this false belief. Because this belief underlies much thinking and description of human events there is a need for a great deal of deconstruction and revision of terminology in our psychological accounts of behaviour.

Notes

1 Symington, Neville (2016). *A Different Path*. London: Karnac Books.
2 Macmurray, John (1957). *The Self as Agent*. p. 11. London: Faber & Faber.
3 Cecil, David (1948). *The Young Melbourne*. p. 265. London: Pan Books Ltd.
4 Rousseau, Jean-Jacques (2013). *Emile*. p. 341. Mineola, NY: Dover Publications.
5 Suttie, Ian D. (1939). *The Origins of Love and Hate*. pp. 4–6. London: Routledge & Kegan Paul & Trench and Trubner & Co. Ltd.
6 Hobson, Peter (2002). *The Cradle of Thought*. p. 178. London: Palgrave Macmillan.

Chapter 4

Consequences of mother's contemplation

At all times sincere friends of freedom have been rare.

—Lord Acton[1]

There is another element in mother's *thinking about her own past experiences in relationships* that is crucial. It is that this activity is entirely free, not something that has been recommended as something good for a mother to do. No midwife or paediatrician has suggested this to the mother. It is an entirely free and spontaneous act. So then the question arises *Why is it that such an act is enabling for the baby?* The surprising answer is that a free act crosses the boundary of the individual and passes into the other – in this case, the baby; so baby and mother are in connection with each other. Baby is *in relation with* mother. The phrase *securely attached* is the wrong mode of description because it distorts the reality of *in relation with*. This is an instance of what was said at the end of the last chapter: that mother and baby are in the shared medium of which the two are a united source of action. It is true that a baby who is in relation with his or her mother is attached securely but this is because the baby is *in relation* and mother and baby are joint actors. A baby *in relation* is secure; a baby not in relation is isolated and insecure. Freedom means that the person in question is not imprisoned and therefore the reflective activity is not held captive within the bounds of the individual's own bodily circumference but is a shared event so what is in one is also in the other. One can see here the huge difference between reflection which has been recommended and reflection which is entirely spontaneous. It is only the latter which has a fruitful consequence for the two participants. This means that if those modes of relating which are recommended in our trainings are followed rather than one's own spontaneous mode of connecting then the understanding of oneself and the other will be distorted.

Freedom and reflecting on experiences, good or bad, are two aspects of the same thing. The essence of reflection is its spontaneity. If it is done under orders it is no longer reflection but deliberation. Deliberation embraces the sense that the emotional activity is under direction. Great strides of innovation occur when the pupil frees himself from his instructor. I give as an example what the biographer says of Raoul Dufy who had been learning in the atelier of his painting teacher in Le Havre who favoured dark sombre portraiture:

> *One day he tried to express all the joy and the light of a beautiful red-haired girl, but was only criticized by his teacher, while the sombre work of one companion was highly praised. Raoul Dufy was then sure that there was nothing else he could learn at that school.*[2]

What was lacking in this man whom I referred to in the last chapter, the one who felt assaulted by an explosive noise when spoken to indicated that his tacit knowledge was undeveloped. It was because this was lacking that speech was experienced as such an assault. Speech not generated by tacit knowledge is like an unexplained loud explosion. This is also so of lectures that are dull and boring.

This is another example: a therapist described how he was able to listen sympathetically to his patients . . . there was however a 'but' in his voice: i.e. something he could not do. What was it? He could not take in the patient's message. He heard the words and tried to use his own experience to sympathize but . . . he could neither take in what was being communicated nor understand. He was seeing a patient together with a colleague and the colleague intuited what the patient was troubled by. He asked the colleague 'How did you manage that?' and she replied 'I had an intuition' – he could hear the words but was not able himself to 'see within.' 'I have truly never taken in anything?' he said, 'I just repeat the words.' So the function whereby the personality takes something in and then intuits from that place was smothered or undeveloped. When this joint dysfunction began to be elucidated the capacity to take in and to intuit began to develop. As soon as something is realized it is a sign that it is already beginning to be transformed. Transformed from what to what? From being a static entity in the personality to an active force within it. Pinocchio changes from being made of wood to being a man of flesh and blood. So this is an example of a therapist whose capacity to take in and then intuit was undeveloped but the process of its development was in progress.

When a spontaneous 'taking in' of her baby by a mother has not happened, there is a characteristic sign of this: the individual becomes attached to the analyst or therapist at the level of sensation – i.e. attached to his voice or her voice, attached to the words of her analyst or therapist.

Functions developed and undeveloped

Professor Matsuzawa of Kyoto University gave chimpanzees and humans an exercise in short-term memory. The chimpanzees did much better than humans. The Professor says:

> *We've concluded through the cognitive tests that chimps have extraordinary memories. They can do things at a glance. As a human you can do*

things to improve your memory, but you will never be a match for Ayuma [a chimpanzee].

Given that humans share 98.8% of their DNA with chimpanzees, why do the latter have such vastly superior working memories?

The answer lies in evolution, says Matsuzawa. As humans evolved and acquired new skills – notably the ability to use language to communicate – they lost others they once shared with their common simian ancestors. 'Our ancestors may have also had photographic memories, but we lost that during evolution so that we could acquire new skills. To get something, we had to lose something.[3]

What has been lost is what Rousseau refers to as the language of expression. This is an interesting perspective on undeveloped functions in the human race generally. Technological advances nearly always mean there is a loss of something. I think the huge increase in terrorism currently is due to an epidemic of poorly formed egos. I think this is because ordinary conversations and the pleasure of companionship occurs much less. What is true of the mother's spontaneous reflection and the consequent companionship existing between mother and baby and how this generates for the baby the capacity to relate to the mother is also true of what occurs between people. The loss of this locus of companionship shows up in an incapacity to take in and retain not only factors in a particular relationship because its scope is much wider – it leads to an inability to respect the freedom to think in many different ways.

I knew a married couple whose capacities were different in this way. The husband was technologically more able than his wife in all matters that concerned machinery. He could take the engine of his car to pieces and reassemble it. He spent a lot of time experimenting with his computer. He had very poor understanding of people. He was puzzled when someone was upset because a friend of his had died. The wife was not technologically capable but, unlike her husband, she had natural understanding of people that she met and understood things that distressed them and things that enhanced their well-being. Companionship was something the husband neither sought, wanted nor understood whereas the wife was the opposite. I suspect therefore that companionship and natural understanding of people are partners; that the companionship generates, like an artist, portraits of other people.

So we gain something through technological discovery but we also lose something. This may contribute to the erosion of crucial functions. Each age, each culture has some functions well developed and others not so. This is so of cultures as well as of individual personalities. This has been stressed by Malcolm Gladwell in his book *Outliers*.[4] It seems that this also implies that the greater the capacity to represent verbally the greater is the loss of more primitive immediate modes of knowledge. So, for instance, the person suffering from psychosis is able to intuit whether the other, the analyst for example, is speaking from his own core or repeating the dictum of another. This raises the question of whether it is right to refer to such a person as being psychotic (i.e. mad) or does it just mean that he does not function in the same way as the majority who have lost 'immediate knowledge' and adopted a substitute: verbal communication. That which is verbal is always further removed from the actual observed happening so, for instance, a painting of a beautiful woman is closer to the woman herself than a verbal description of her. Rousseau says this:

> *By neglecting the language of expression we have lost the most forcible mode of speech. The spoken word is always weak, and we speak to the heart rather through the eyes then the ears.*[5]

I have given some examples. I want now to look at the capacities themselves and to realize that they are often undeveloped.

Ability to suffer pain

There is pain which is suffered and pain which is raw or unsuffered. 'Suffering pain' we equate with taking the pain inside and allowing it to permeate the functioning mind. The clinician's job therefore is to act in such a way as to promote the capacity to suffer. If pain is not suffered it is expelled. A woman was unable to tolerate her child state of mind. She was chronologically a grown woman so she found it unbearable to bear witness to the fact that she was, although aged 50, yet a baby in her sensibilities. How did she deal with the pain of seeing in this way? By utterly eradicating the seer from her world. Whenever she saw him, the one who knew her history even from afar, she fled and hid herself.

By 'him' is meant any figure that could remind her of her child state of mind. So, for instance, when she saw in a supermarket an elderly teacher whom she had known at school thirty-five years before it sent her into a panic.

When pain is not suffered it lives as a raw force producing anxiety which has mental manifestations and bodily ones. When we say it produces anxiety it does not mean that the individual is aware of being anxious; what is being referred to are actions which damage like an addiction to drugs or a compulsion to neatness or a need to impose his or her own mode of action upon another or languishing in a state of despair. This raw force can find shelter in a school of thinking, an ideology or a religious belief but the personality is left impoverished because this force is used against it as an enemy rather than being a friendly ally. The good things that occur are infiltrated with this distorting force, making what could be fruitful into something harmful.

When pain is not suffered it is expelled into the body, into people in the social environment, usually people who are intimate. It is also frequently expelled into a school of thinking, into an ideology or a religious belief but the personality is left impoverished because of this expulsion and therefore a negativity permeates the personality. The good things that occur are not known and certainly not enjoyed.

Pain suffered enriches the personality; pain expelled impoverishes the personality. This is a truth which has been emphasized in many religious spiritualities down the ages.

Bill Clinton in the introduction to Mandela's book *Long Walk to Freedom* says this:

> *I said, 'Tell me the truth. When you were leaving prison after twenty-seven years and walking down that road to freedom, didn't you hate them all over again?' And he said, 'Absolutely I did, because they had imprisoned me for so long, I was abused. I didn't get to see my children grow up. I lost my marriage and the best years of my life. I was angry. And I was afraid, because I had not been free in so long. But as I got closer to the car that would take me away, I realized that when I went through that gate, if I still hated them, they would still have me. I wanted to be free. And so I let it go.*⁶

But how is that change of heart achieved? It is the capacity to achieve this in small things and great that enriches and develops the personality. The clinician cannot make someone have such a change of heart but is there a way in which its possibility can be fostered? I believe that the way that makes it most probable is through the clinician's own reflective inner acts. Just after the First World War Wittgenstein in companionship with his friend Engelmann engaged in a kind of a reflective self-confession. Engelmann wrote to Wittgenstein expressing his own confessional experience and this enabled Wittgenstein to surface his own self-confession. This is how it is recorded:

> *Behind such thoughts, just as in others, there can probably lie something of a noble motive. But that this motive shows itself in this way, that it takes the form of a contemplation of suicide, is certainly wrong. Suicide is certainly a mistake. So long as person lives, he is never completely lost. What drives a man to suicide is, however, the fear that he is completely lost. This fear is, in view of what has already been said, ungrounded. In this fear a person does the worst thing he can do, he deprives himself of the time in which it would be possible for to escape being lost.*
>
> *And then he goes on:*
> *'You undoubtedly know all this better than I . . . but one sometimes forgets what one knows.'*
> *The biographer continues:*
> *On this occasion, however, it was not the advice that did him good, but simply reading about Engelmann's own efforts.*⁷

This is what was meant by Bion when he counselled analysts to be present in the consulting-room without memory or desire – in other words to be there just with his or her own raw self and to be rid of all extraneous implants. Mandela realized that hatred of his prison guards would keep him captive but, in his case, it was a heroism which is rare.

When the attempt is made to banish pain the personality is impoverished. Painful happenings are part of life so to put energy into eroding pain is, at the same time, a subversion of life itself. When the attempt is made to evacuate the pain then there is no personal growth because acceptance of pain enriches the personality. If however the pain is received and shared then a transformation occurs. Instead of the personality being deprived it is enriched. There is no life deprived of painful occurrences. I cannot, at birth, declare that I will be prepared to live as long as I have a guarantee against pain. As I am walking one day I stumble and break my arm; when I am just twelve my mother and father are killed in a train crash; my great hope in life was to become a doctor but my examination results were not good enough so I did not get into medical school. Yet by a strange enigma whenever a disaster occurs it opens up a new possibility. One door is shut and others open. By transformation we refer to this opening up of other doors. So when a painful happening occurs the person is required to view the new situation into which life has plunged him.

Shame – knowledge (negative transference)

There is a knowing of those functions which are undeveloped at the same time as hiding from what is known. I have quoted in the last chapter that statement where Lord Melbourne makes clear that it is these 'faults of nature' that people are ashamed of.[8] Shame consists therefore of two contradictories: knowledge of a handicap in body or mind and, at the same time, a shrinking away from this knowledge. When a function is undeveloped it also means the ego is stunted because the ego creates from a synthesis of all the functions. If one function is undeveloped it enfeebles the whole ego. This hiding of what is known which is the core of shame is what fashions Freud's Unconscious and distinguishes it from the Preconscious. The former is the consequence of an active turning away from what is unformed; the latter arises when attention is upon one thing and therefore not on another and this 'other' is what Freud called *Preconscious*. If that undeveloped function is identified this observational process protects the ego which is then able to gain in strength. The identification is not just 'seeing' it but rather a constructive act.

What is the reason for this 'shrinking away from the fact of the handicap'? I think it comes from our ancestral heritage. What I mean is this: that in the tribal unit, in the hominid band, the damaged or imperfect one is killed or eliminated. So shame is the receiver of this heritage. In shame there is a turning away from the sight of the damaged self because it invites elimination. A man I once treated who had a club foot spoke frequently of the way a flock of birds would peck to death the damaged member of the flock. Therefore there is a sense that if I am damaged I shall be done to death so shame is the emotion that hides the damage first from myself and then from others and yet the fact of shame reveals that there is something that requires some mending.

What though is the consequence of an undeveloped function that is known? Does awareness of this alter things? Quite simply it keeps the damage within the perimeter of the handicapped organ and thus protects the whole personality from being held in contempt. Therefore the clinician's job is to find the damaged part and bring it to light and thus protect the whole personality from a poisonous infection. The damaged function is poisonous when it is not known, not attended to; it can be enhancing when it is known. It is enhancing because then it is possible for someone to see the good things on the credit side of the balance sheet and also the bad things on the debit side and this knowledge of the good gives confidence to the person and also this confidence is combined with humility.

Shame consists therefore of two contradictories: knowledge of a handicap in body or mind and, at the same time, a shrinking away from it. Freud's concept of repression and resistance was a way of describing shame in terms of his instinct theory. When Freud formulated the notion of repression and resistance he was taking shame as it had been formulated by philosophers and theologians for centuries and placing it within a scientific instinctual schema.

Envy as a consequence of shame

I think the emphasis upon envy within psycho-analysis shields us from what it is that generates envy: i.e. the absence, deformation or unformation of a crucial function. I become envious when I see in another the presence of a function which I lack, or believe I lack, in myself. In the Monastery of San Martín in Puebla de Sanábria in the Asturias in northern Spain there is on the outer wall the following inscription:

Let us occupy ourselves not with envying others but with finding in ourselves that which we envy.

The word 'find' needs to be given an active creative sense. I may not have the same developed function as I perceive in another but I find some trace of it and turn attention to it. This attention has a fertilizing effect. I may realize that this is not so well developed in me and maybe it never will be as well developed as in this other but if I follow the advice on that monastery wall I will find another. We would not want a world where all had the same gifts. It is a variety of gifts that makes for a fruitful community.

There is another component. What is referred to as envy implies too great a focus upon the other. If we apply ourselves to the revealing of images within then we shall be closer to the person that we are with. If we attend to our own frustration rather than the intention of the other then we shall be closer to the truth about the other. I think this makes sense of the remark attributed to Bion that is often quoted as a joke when he says to his patient:

'I don't know why you are so angry with me; I am not trying to help you.'

He was not focussed on the other but to elements in himself; elements undeveloped, developing or an inner factor evolving. There is an implication here: that a state of mind in oneself, once attended to and brought into awareness, transmits to the other. In other words to focus on the other is an obstacle to this transmission because it takes attention away from the place where it needs to be: on this element inside of me. Once attention to this is established the transmission to the other happens automatically.

Aggregate delusion

The ego sees the outer world, especially the social world, according to the way in which it itself is constituted. We have a deep seated assumption that our ego is individual but frequently we are merged into an aggregate social lump. So that the category 'all men' or 'all women,' 'all doctors' or 'all psycho-analysts,' 'all Australians' or 'all Japanese' are what constitutes the ego.[9] This partly arises in conjunction with an undeveloped function and therefore a weakened ego which can only find strength by agglomerating itself. This aggregate delusion is correlated with the super-ego which is always embodied in such an agglomeration. So the ego thus agglomerated sees not individuals but persons as agglomerated categories. In fact the aggregate delusion is an exposition of the super-ego. If I were asked 'Well what is the super-ego?' then I would say it is when the aggregate delusion smothers my own autonomous self. The transference then in such a delusion is not to the analyst as an individual but as a solidified lump undifferentiated from others in his or her category. The fact that the analyst is perceived through such a lens indicates that the patient him- or herself is not a person but a solidified lump. (It is, I believe, a safe proposition that I see the other through the lens of my own elements of which I am unaware.) Jung's elaboration of 'individuation' gives helpful insight here.[10] He describes psychologically how the individual separates out from the mass, from the lump.

Example 1: A man would say 'You disapprove of my CBT practice.' This was untrue. I have no objection to CBT. He said this because Neville is a psycho-analyst and psycho-analysts disapprove of CBT, so he believes. It may be true that some psycho-analysts do but it has become a dogmatic assertion and attributed to every psycho-analyst.

Example 2: An elderly woman believed that Freud's idea that civilization was repressive of individual desire was wrong but that I would scorn her for this view of hers. In fact I was in complete agreement.

Both these examples indicate that these patients believed I was in a 'black and white' merged state – that there was no individual relationship to psycho-analysis or to Freud. The idea that I might agree with some psycho-analytic attitudes but not others or some of Freud's theoretical formulations but not others was not in her mind. My selfhood was in an attached, glue-like, state. The reason however why these two patients saw me in this mode is that they were in that mode themselves. There was not an individual creative person *in relation* to group ideals.

There is a hidden delusion here. It arises out of this passive state. Why is this? I think it is because a delusion, like an hallucination, is the consequence of a discharge. This suggests that the element in the personality that effects the delusion is hated. And why? Because instead of incorporating an element and creating it so that it can enrich the personality it is discharged and therefore robs me of my own being. The core of my being, if fully developed, is free so I hate that which destroys my most inward self, this precious treasure within.

Nature of understanding

We are interested to know how the delusional system can be dissolved. I believe it occurs through an act of understanding but this has to be personal rather than vicarious. It is vicarious when it is an act of understanding derived from someone else. That someone else may be Freud, Jung, Melanie Klein, Kohut, Winnicott, Bion, Balint or any other thinker. It may be the dictate of a supervisor. If the other has given expression, like an accurate interpretation, of something that is personal then it is no longer vicarious. We all have in us aggregate delusions. When we reach them in ourselves we free ourselves from the bondage of uniformity and come into personal enlightenment. The reason for this is that then there is an 'I' seeing the aggregate delusion so that 'I' is not immersed and submerged inside of the aggregate delusion.

Personal connection

It is because the individual person is entrapped in an aggregate that he/she is subject to beliefs like: I don't believe I exist, I believe I am immortal, I believe I am dead, I believe I am god, I believe when I die that the universe will come to an end, I believe that no one exists other than myself and I believe I created the world to serve my needs. It can be seen that these delusions sort themselves out into two general classes: either that I do not exist at all or that I and no other thing exists. In the first category the aggregate delusion has smothered the 'I' or strangled it so that it cannot function so there is a truth in the statement 'I don't exist.' In the second case it is not the 'I' that has been eliminated but everything except the 'I' but when this is looked at closely it can be seen that the so-called 'I' is really a misnomer. What is being called 'I' is an aggregate delusion. The individual who thinks that when he or she dies the world will come to an end does so because again there is a certain truth: when he or she dies it is not a person dying while the rest of the world continues but an aggregate delusional 'I' that comes to an end. Either of these basic delusions are substitutes for an undeveloped function. What function? A separate individual 'I' that imagines, thinks and judges. A delusion is always a substitute for an undeveloped function and these two prime delusions occur because the most fundamental function is undeveloped – i.e. the creative principle that is the core of the personality.

A very important delusion is the belief that I am a piece of wood. I am inanimate. This delusion, like all delusions, has strong philosophical, psychological and psychiatric support. The view that we are all determined by stimuli from outside arises from this delusion. But this is a delusion that holds sway in much scientific thought and philosophical theorizing and is epitomized in Francis Crick's book *The Astonishing Hypothesis*. The reason for stressing this is that delusions can encompass a whole culture and its thinking. Erich Fromm said that we are familiar with the idea of a *folie à deux* but he said there can also be a *folie à millions*.[11] The importance of this is that in the individual in his/her core there may be a sane striving to become who they are but if they have ingested beliefs from the culture which do not truly belong to the core self then the endeavour will fail.

There is a theme running through the chapters of this book. This has been lucidly expressed by Marion Milner. She says:

> *It was quite clear to me, for instance, that the ideas I was discovering must have wide psycho-analytic implications. The reason why I did not at any time make the attempt to express what I saw in terms of conventional psycho-analytic concepts was that I wanted to keep rigidly within the bounds of my own actual observation, to try as far as possible to forget everything I had read, everything I had been told, and to assume nothing that did not emerge out of my own direct experience. . . . This did not mean that I under-estimated the value of psycho-analytic knowledge, small or great, it only meant that I had come to the firm conclusion that reading must come after one had learnt the tricks for observing one's mind, not before; since if it comes before it is only too easy to accept technical concepts intellectually and use them as jargon, not as instruments for the real understanding of experience.*[12]

Many years ago I took into treatment a mentally handicapped man. He was aged 33 and had an IQ of 59. I had been told that psycho-analytic psychotherapy could only work with someone who had an IQ of over 100. I had something in me of Marion Milner's mistrust of edicts of this nature so I took him on and remarkable changes occurred in him. Two or three years later when I was at the Tavistock I proposed to start a workshop on the treatment of mentally handicapped patients. At the time Alexis Brook was the Chairman at the Tavistock and encouraged me with great enthusiasm to start this workshop so, together with six colleagues we started off. However the senior psychologist in the Adult Department instructed us, prior to taking on any such patients, to read for a whole year the literature on the subject of treatment of the mentally handicapped. This instruction I firmly disobeyed and instead agreed with my colleagues that we would learn about mental handicap by actually encountering such patients and coming to know them.

Notes

1 Acton, John Emerich Edward Dalberg-Acton. *The History of Freedom & Other Essays*. p. 1. London: Macmillan & Co.
2 Cogniat, Raymond (1978). *Raoul Dufy*. pp. 14–15. Naefels, Switzerland: Bonfini Press Corporation.
3 Article written by Justin McCurry in *The Guardian Weekly* of 11.10.13.

4 Gladwell, Malcolm (2008). *Outliers*. Penguin Books.
5 Rousseau, Jean-Jacques (2013). *Emile*. p. 341. Mineola, NY: Dover Publications.
6 Mandela, Nelson (2013). *Long Walk to Freedom*. pp. ix–x. New York: Abacus & Imprint of Little Brown Book Group.
7 Monk, Ray (1990). *Ludwig Wittgenstein*. p. 187. New York: The Free Press & Maxwell Macmillan.
8 'It wounds a man less to confess that he has failed in any pursuit through idleness, neglect, the love of pleasure, etc., etc., which are his own faults, than through incapacity and unfitness, which are the fault of his nature.' Cecil, David (1948). *The Young Melbourne*. p. 265. London: Pan Books Ltd.
9 This is consistent with Matte Blanco's theory of infinite sets. See Matte Blanco, Ignacio (1975). *The Unconscious as Infinite Sets – An Essay in Bi-Logic*. London: Gerald Duckworth and Co & Matte Blanco, Ignacio (1988). *Thinking, Feeling and Being*. New Library of Psychoanalysis. London & New York: Routledge (A Tavistock Professional Book).
10 Jung, C.G. (1975). The Archetypes and the Collective Unconscious. In *The Collected Works of C.G. Jung* – vol 9, part I. pp. 290–354.
11 Fromm, Erich (1972). *Psychoanalysis and Religion*. p. 16. Toronto, New York & London: Bantam Books.
12 Field, Joanna (Marion Milner) (1986). *A Life of One's Own*. p. 202. London: Virago Press.

Chapter 5

Hypnotic power

It is often thought that hypnotism is a phenomenon confined to the hypnotist's consulting-room. Tolstoy, in his essay *The Kingdom of God*, said that this power is much more widespread. He says:

> *The difference between men artificially hypnotized and those under the influence of governmental suggestion consists in this – that to the former their imagined environment is suggested suddenly by one person, and the suggestion operates only for a short time; whereas to the latter, their imagined position has been the result of gradual suggestion, going on, not for years, but for generations, and proceeds not from a single individual, but their entire circumstances.*[1]

What needs to be added to what he says is that those who are hypnotized by some group institutional belief are not aware that they are in this hypnotized state. They go along unquestioningly with what the government, institution or school of thinking has declared to be the truth. In fact most of our factual knowledge, or so-called factual knowledge, is derived from authoritative statements which we have learnt first from our parents and relatives before we went to school, then from teachers at school and then from lecturers at university. A goal of this book is to stimulate us all to observe what happens and then to give expression to our experience. I quoted in the last chapter the statement of Marion Milner of which the key sentence is:

> *I wanted to keep rigidly within the bounds of my own actual observation, to try as far as possible to forget everything I had read, everything I had been told, and to assume nothing that did not emerge out of my own direct experience.*[2]

In a later work of hers, *On Not Being Able to Paint* she says that when painting she knew that what she had to do was to bring out from her own inner soul a creation that was entirely hers but the temptation to copy the design of another was a powerful and insistent force that thrust itself upon her and which she had to resist. This is what she says when considering the contemplative mood required for artistic originality.

> *The essential thing about this contemplative mood, combined with action, was that it involved me in a giving up of the wish to make an exact reproduction of anything I had seen. Since obviously one cannot anyway produce a truly realistic copy of any object known in the external world, for marks on a two-dimensional surface can never be an exact reproduction of a three-dimensional object, it would seem that this was not a very difficult wish to give up. Nevertheless, in spite of my early discovery that no attempt to copy the appearance of objects was what my eye liked there was still a continual inner battle to be waged against the urge to attempt this mechanical copying; and this, in spite of years of experience of the fact that it was only when I had discarded this wish to copy that the resulting drawing or painting had any life in it, any of the sense of a living integrated structure existing in its own right. Of course I knew that many of the greatest artists said that they did copy nature, but I had begun to doubt whether this really meant what it seemed to mean. I began to suspect that they were in fact trying to describe the process of surrendering themselves to the deep spontaneous responses of nature within them, that were stimulated by the contact with nature outside them.*[3]

To see the world as it is and not as we have been instructed to see it is extremely difficult. Bernard Berenson, the famous art critic, who was mentor and teacher of Kenneth Clark says this:[4]

> *the most difficult thing in the world is to see clearly and with one's own eyes, naïvely. . . . Only when a person is to become an artist is a systematic effort made to teach him. But note how it is done. . . . He was set to copy simple drawings of his own master, or of other artists. Then the antique was put before him, and he had to copy that. By this time his habits of vision were well on the way to becoming fixed, and, unless he were endowed with unusual powers of reacting against teaching, he passed the rest of his life seeing in objects only those shapes and forms that the drawings and antiques put before him had pointed out to him. . . . And, unless years devoted to the study of all schools of art have taught us to see with our own eyes, we soon fall into the habit of moulding whatever we look at into the forms borrowed from the one art with which we are acquainted.*

So here are two people, immersed in the art world, telling us that it is extremely difficult to see what is actually there in front of us and then to act in accordance with what has been seen. It is easier to do what I am told to see than to repudiate that and see what *I* see. Why is this? In order to answer this we need to pursue more closely the hypnotic phenomenon.

So in what exactly does this hypnotic power consist? It is clear that the individual 'gives over' his or her own power of judgement into the guidance of another. It seems that there is an elemental fear of being steward of one's own conduct. If I make a judgement that comes entirely from the inner estimate of my own observation I cannot do this without realizing that I may be wrong. It seems that there is a powerful desire to know that what has been asserted is definitely right. This explains, it would seem, the glue-like attachment we make to the doctrines of the Catholic Church, to the doctrine of reincarnation as taught within Buddhism, to the central tenets of psycho-analysis. These are always proclaimed with certainty. It is less frightening to hand over the management of one's life to another who proclaims first that he or she knows and secondly that what he or she knows is right. We don't like to live according to inner principles which may not be right. We like certainty without doubt but certainty without doubt is dogmatism and terrorism. And yet there is a paradox here: why is this 'other' trusted and not oneself? The way this question is put suggests that the answer lies in something rational yet the abdication of one's own judgement and submission to that of another is not based on any rational procedure. What is considered to be one unitary act is in fact made up of two processes. The first is the fear of one's own judgement so one's own judgement is renounced. This renunciation of one's own judgement, one's own soul, leaves the individual in a dead-like state. He becomes a machine-tool ready to be used according to the objectives of another. He renounces personhood and becomes a functionary.

This psychological act whereby the individual abandons his own creative essence and power to choose for himself is driven by fear. But fear of what? To adopt a position which is the outcome of his own creative act, one where he makes a choice, puts him in a place where he can blame no one for his situation in life. It is one that he has chosen. He becomes a focus for the emotions of others. These emotions may be hostile or friendly but that it will draw towards him the intense emotional force of others is certain. Also he is taking a stand upon an inner figment of the imagination while not knowing whether this is correct or not and this cannot be determined by the response of others. Some may admire the position he has taken; others may hate it or oppose it vigorously. He may never know whether what he did was right. This is a potent reason for evading an issue where he has to make his own judgement. Not to have certainty about whether the life-choice someone has made is right is a difficult thing to live with.

The hypnotist can only be effective if he or she reigns in a region that is superior, or thought to be superior, to the individual or individuals being hypnotized. There is in human beings a vulnerable open-ness to the bright light of supremacy. Tolstoy, in *War and Peace*, gives voice to this when he describes Nikolai Rostov's surrendering devotion to the Emperor, Emperor Alexander. He willingly puts himself into the most dangerous unit of the battle because this will give him the chance of taking a message from General Bagration to the Emperor. It will give him the chance of *seeing* the Emperor. To be able to please this supreme figure is the prime motivating factor in his inner decisions. Within the Judaeo-Christian-Islamic tradition the figure of 'God' holds this supremacy. And then within each of these three religious traditions there is a figure that is sacred and special to that particular one. So in Judaism it is God but in particular his choice of the Israelites as his special favourites upon the earth with the rescue of the people from Egypt and the crossing of the Red Sea as the saving event with Moses as the deliverer. In Christianity it is Jesus who is the supreme hypnotizer and the saving event being in the Resurrection of Christ and in Islam it is Muhammad and the record of his message from God in the Koran with the Hegira as the saving event. In all these cases the figure in question exists totally apart and above the swarming mass of mankind.

The Ultimate, the Infinite, is Existence itself. A marvel, which is outside any scientific category, is Existence itself. We do not know how Existence came to be. Science is able to examine particular aspects of this Existence. Astronomers study the stars and the planets; entomologists study insects, geologists study the formation and structure of our planet; botanists study plant life; zoologists study animal life. All these are particular segments of Existence but Existence itself cannot be understood in this way. Judaism, Christianity and Islam say that it was God who created Existence, who created the Universe but then who created God? It was Moses Maimonides who was the first constructor of what has become known as the *Via Negativa*. He was pointing to this Ultimate, this Infinity by saying 'It is *not* the stars, it is *not* the stones, rocks and earth of our planet, it is *not* the plant life, it is *not* the animal life.' It is not any particular division of the whole but Existence itself that is the object attended to. If this is truly grasped then all systems of thought, be they religious, scientific or aesthetic are only therefore particular manifestations of this Ultimate. What leads to distortion, to fanaticism, to terrorism is when what is a manifestation is made into an Ultimate. As soon as it is said that Buddhism, Christianity or Psycho-analysis is the ultimate then stupidity, ignorance and massive grandiosity occupy the mental world of its devotees.

The psycho-analyst is frequently viewed by the patient as someone who is a superior being, someone who is above the ordinary problems and predicaments of human beings. The question is how is this illusion to be undone? Recently an experience occurred that gives some food for thought. The patient had a poor opinion of himself, blamed himself for some bad decisions he had taken in his life. Then a noticeable change occurred. He began to trust his own judgements; began to see good things in *his* life; began *not* to think that what another did had to be better than what he did. This change in direction was noticeable. What had brought this about? The analyst had written an autobiography in which it was clear that he had made some serious choices in life, or more accurately, gone in certain directions, which were disastrous. The patient read this book. So 'Oh' he thought 'it is not only me that has made blunders in my life.' He was with an analyst who also had. So here he was with an analyst who had made blunders but nevertheless recovered sufficiently to lead a reasonably fruitful life. 'So maybe I can also lead a fruitful life in the future.' The analyst had been removed from being the Ultimate upon Earth.

It is my thesis that this submission to another, whether it be an individual or an institution, arises from a single person's primordial fear of standing on his own ground and judging from it. After Copernicus but before Johannes Kepler astronomers and the scientific world of the time believed that the planets circulated the sun in perfect circles but Kepler, with his telescope in Prague, tracked the orbit of Mars and then knew that its track around the sun was not circular but elliptical. But it took him six years before he dared to declare it openly. The whole world believed that the planets went around the sun in perfect circles and to stand up and defy this belief was a frightening thing to do. It was also dangerous with the religious authorities. In Kepler's case it was the elders in the Lutheran hierarchy. Arthur Koestler says there was some comforting sense in believing that the planets went round the sun in perfect circles. Kepler threw a bomb-shell into this satisfying belief. It had been the same with Galileo. Galileo's championing of heliocentrism was controversial during his lifetime when most subscribed to geocentrism. The matter was investigated by the Roman Inquisition in 1615 which concluded that heliocentrism was 'foolish and absurd in philosophy and formally heretical' since it explicitly contradicts in many places the statements in Holy Scripture. He was tried by the Inquisition and found 'vehemently suspect of heresy' and forced to recant and spent the rest of his life under house arrest.

We may look upon these authorities, in one case the Lutheran hierarchy with Kepler and in the other the Roman Catholic Church with Galileo, with a superior contempt all the while not realizing that we are today also under the auspices, the authority, of systems of thinking that seem so natural, so obviously part of reality that we do not question it. This is why when Tolstoy says we are all in this hypnotized state it is true but to the hypnotizing gurus of these systems of thought there is a hatred of any questioning of the doctrinal positions with which they have inoculated their disciples.

So this open-ness to the bright of supremacy has dangers, serious dangers. Once a figure is invested with this power and submitted to then it is capable of huge destruction. To submit entirely, to renounce your own judgement and replace it with total obedience to the authority of another is, in itself, a dangerous procedure. To start with it is a renunciation of one's own subjective assessment of a proposition or a system of propositions. It is like blinding oneself so that one can no longer see the way to go. It is this act of self-blinding that is precarious. The guide into whose care one puts oneself is subject to error. He or she does not know what is right for you; he or she does not know the workings of your own mind or the project that you are engaged with. Through this renunciation of one's own judgement one becomes a robot that is in obedience and one that is unable to assess whether this path along which you are being led is the right one.

The state of being in love is *the* prototype of this giving of oneself over to another. This happens when a man falls in love with a woman or a woman falls in love with a man or a man with a man, or a woman with a woman. This phenomenon so elemental, so well-known to everyone in the world, is yet mysterious. Quite what is it that leads a man to 'fall in love'? What is it about the woman that elicits this giving over of himself to her? What is it that makes her wonderful, all-consuming, filling his world with no thoughts other than her? Every movement, every utterance that comes from her is endowed with a bright light of wonder. What is this? How does it come about? Sexual desire is an important component but it does not encompass or explain the whole of it. A desire for sexual satisfaction is more general. Several women could present themselves to a man and arouse in him sexual desire but he would not be in love. Uniqueness is the essential additional component of this state of being in love. This person and no other evokes a passionate commitment to this one and this one alone. It seems that the loved one has assumed into herself a transcendence that is beyond her. It seems then that there is a something that transcends the world of sensation that has the power to magnetize the individual to this absolute.

There is a pull from the heavens upon human beings – a tug from the infinite. All religions and ideologies attest to this fact: that an ultimate, an infinite has an attracting force upon the minds and hearts of human beings. It is able to pull someone into its precincts. When the unknown, the infinite, is located mentally where it belongs then all phenomena are manifestations of it. Fanaticism, terrorism and fundamentalism occur when what is a phenomenon, that which is a manifestation of the infinite, claims that it is itself the infinite. It is no longer a signal pointing to the infinite but declares that it itself *is* the infinite. The Christian religion says that it itself is the Truth, Islam makes the same claim as also does Judaism. All different religious denominations made for themselves similar claims. This is so also of Buddhism. It is also so of all the subdivisions within any of these religions. So within Christianity, Catholics say that they have the Truth; Protestants say that they have the truth; within Islam the Sunnis claim to have the truth as do also the Shias. It is similar in Judaism between the Orthodox and Reformed. Within Buddhism the many different strands from Theravada, Mahayana or Tantric claim, each of them, to be the possessor of the truth. Only the mystics (and not the false mystics) know that the infinite transcends all the manifestations of Being. The mystic knows that a particular religious denomination is one pathway to the truth but that there are others. This does not mean that all pathways are equally truth-carrying but that the mystic knows that any one religious system is never more than a *pathway* to the infinite.

What has been said here of religious denominations is also so of secular ideologies, like Communism, Freemasonry or Psycho-Analysis. Each of these claims to be *the* way to utopia. Melanie Klein said that utopia would arrive when all people had been analyzed; it was thought that perfect bliss would have been achieved when Communism had been established in all the lands.

But the question is 'How is it that the infinite' has this tug upon creatures? The clue lies in the fact that it does not have this *tug* upon a true mystic. A mystic, like Meister Eckhart, knew that this Existence, this Infinity, was in him. He was it. He did not have to go racing after something outside himself because he knew that it already existed at the centre of himself. What had he done that gave him this knowledge? He detached himself from the world of sensation. He had arrived at the knowledge that he was participating in the Infinite and therefore this rather than his human bodily being was the manifestation of this Ultimate. Meister Eckhart puts it clearly thus:

> *why I praise detachment more than humility is that perfect humility bows down beneath all creatures, and in this bending down man goes out of himself and into the creatures. But detachment remains within itself. Now no going out can ever be so noble as the indwelling is in itself.*[5]

This going out to find the Infinite in creatures, in a world of delusion, was what he did not do.

So the hypnotic phenomenon is first when what is a *manifestation* of the infinite becomes invested with infinite qualities and then someone submits to it. One sees this when something is claimed to be true because Freud said it, or Jung said it or Karl Marx said it or Sartre said it or Aristotle or Plato said it. Because one of these great thinkers said it then it *must* be true. Yet the Truth itself is always *beyond*; what Freud, Jung or Marx said are particular manifestations of the Truth. All manifestations of the Truth are mixed in with matters that are not true. All thinkers, however great, have had their glimpses of Truth embodied in contexts that are not true or only true within a limited time-frame. So once someone is in submission to a great thinker, whether it be Aristotle or Freud, he or she is renouncing his or her own subjective judgement in favour of an authority that is fated to be faulty. Is there any way in which someone can be faithful to the Truth? What is being implied here is that the exercise of a person's own inner subjective judgement is the guarantor of Truth yet this cannot be so. If Aristotle or Freud were unable to embody the whole of Truth, the whole of Infinity, then this is so of every individual so if I, this someone, makes a judgement or perceives a Truth it is only a manifestation and therefore a mixture of Truth and untruth. But is there any advantage of a judgement from *me* that is only a partial truth? Why is my partial truth any better than the partial truth of Freud or Aristotle? It is that the expression of a partial truth enunciated by myself is better than a truth that was enunciated by Freud. It is, as Mcneile Dixon said:

> *All philosophies are in the end personal. You can no more escape your philosophy than you can escape your own shadow, for it is also a reflection of yourself*[6]

so in the end every enunciated truth is personal. This means that a truth enunciated by Freud was right for Freud; that there was in it a glimpse of *the* Truth combined with a manifestation that conformed to the 'shape' of Freud himself but to no one else. It does not mean that others were not inspired by his insights as they were. His disciples are well-known: Abraham, Ferenczi, Jones, Ranke and others but, even when we examine these we find that there were subtle differences between the way they thought and conceptualized things and the way of their Master and sometimes these personal divergences from Freud erupted into violent opposition. This was clearly so with Jung, with Adler and, to a lesser extent, with Ferenczi and Ranke.

* * *

When someone's subjectivity is intact and he is *in relation* to Freud (or to Klein, Kohut, Lacan or Winnicott) then the hypnotic circumstance does not happen, cannot happen. When the person's own soul is actively engaged with the mind of the other, whether it be Freud, Jung or Plato, then there is an interaction, an inspired incentive occurring in this shared unity which produces startling new images and thoughts. These come about through this interplay between the two persons. There is an open-ness between the two. There is a particular state of mind that is a signal of this intercourse between the united pair. The core of the mind is a creator and that what is therapeutic for both parties are the myths generated by the mind's core. These myths, these imaginings of the idle mind, have an effect that changes the inner orientation and outer direction. Whereas when one of the pair was in submission to an ingested authority now this is effaced in favour of a dream-like union of minds. Marion Milner referred to this state as a *wide-unfocussed stare*:

> *I myself had learnt when writing the Joanna Field books, for instance, about having observed that there were two kinds of attention, both necessary, a wide unfocused stare, and a narrow focused penetrating kind, and that the wide kind brought remarkable changes in perception and enrichment of feeling.*[7]

She quotes Elton Mayo who, while at Harvard Business School, wrote an article on *reverie* where he distinguished between directed thinking and undirected thinking saying that the aim of former was to establish truths whereas the latter was to construct relationships. So the point here is that hypnotism shuts out, prevents the intercourse between two separate minds coming into union with one another. What it does is to make one mental orientation obliterate all others. Marion Milner had a realization of this and expressed it thus:

> *While attending the training seminars during the blitz and the blackout, there was a phrase lurking in the back of my mind, something to do with Samuel Butler having said that a misgiving is a warning from God to be attended to as a man values his soul. Indeed I tried to keep a diary of misgivings about the theory I was trying to learn and when I came to give seminars myself I sometimes advised my students to do the same.*[8]

Although not referring to the phenomenon of hypnotism explicitly she is here warning herself to be on the alert not to let this submission to an authority intrude and destroy imagination and thought. This *submission to authority* is what hypnotism is. As Tolstoy says in the quote which I give at the beginning, this surrender is not to an individual but to a government and that it has been going on for generations; that we are all subject to this hypnotic power invested not only in a political ideologies like socialism or conservatism but also in religious denominations such as Judaism, Christianity or Hinduism and secular schools of thinking such as Behaviourism or Psycho-Analysis. Within psycho-analysis there are ideological schools such as Self Psychology, Klein theory, Lacanian ideals, Classical Freud theory. All these schools of thinking have their devotees: people who are in hypnotic surrender to a system. *Schools of thinking* is not correct because *thinking* is the process whereby a personal experience is transformed from raw impulse into the calmness of a vision seen through the eyes of the world. The transformation is of something within an isolated bubble into something seen as a manifestation of the ultimate. The paradox is that because it is now seen as a manifestation of the ultimate it becomes a faithful creation of this individual's mind and mental attitude.

Bion supported this idea when he said that the analyst needed to be in a state without memory or desire, emphasizing that it was this conscious presumption that got in the way of unfocussed attention.[9] Freud, in different and less concise language, had said exactly the same thing. Bion today is often quoted but Freud's statements seem forgotten. For that reason I quote what Freud says:

> *as soon as anyone deliberately concentrates his attention to a certain degree, he begins to select from the material before him; one point will be fixed in his mind with particular clearness and some other will be correspondingly disregarded, and in making this selection he will be following his expectations or inclinations. This, however, is precisely what must not be done. In making this selection, if he follows his expectations he is in danger of never finding anything but what he already knows; and if he follows his inclinations he will certainly falsify what he may perceive.*[10]

We are talking of an emotional activity that fertilizes the two people who are engaged with one another. It is this inner natural *idleness of mind* that inspires, that crystallizes and illuminates problems.

Notes

1. Tolstoi, L.N. The Kingdom of God. In *The Complete Works of Lyof N. Tolstoi*. p. 297. New York: Thomas Y. Crowell Company.
2. Field, Joanna (Marion Milner) (1986). *A Life of One's Own*. p. 202. London: Virago Press.
3. Milner, Marion (1984). *On Not Being Able to Paint*. pp. 153–154. London: Heinemann.
4. Berenson, Bernard (1954). *The Italian Painters of the Renaissance*. p. 105. London: The Phaidon Press.
5. Meister Eckhart (1963). *Selected Treatises and Sermons*. p. 157. New York: Harper-Collins & Fontana Library.

6 Mcneile Dixon, W. (1958). *The Human Situation.* p. 13. Penguin Books.
7 Milner, Marion (1987). *The Suppressed Madness of Sane Men.* [The Framed Gap]. p. 81. London & New York: Tavistock Publications.
8 Milner, Marion (1987). *The Suppressed Madness of Sane Men.* p. 9. [Introduction]. London & New York: Tavistock Publications.
9 Bion, W.R. (1974). *Bion's Brazilian Lectures.* vol.1. p. 50. Rio de Janeiro: Imago Editora Ltda.
10 Freud, S. (1912). *Recommendations to Physicians Practising Psycho-Analysis.* S.E.v.XII. pp. 111–112. London: The Hogarth Press & The Institute of Psycho-Analysis.

Chapter 6

Unfocussed stare

In a seminar given by Bion to the Klein group at the Institute of Psycho-Analysis in London in July 1978 he said:

Most psycho-analysts do not believe that this strange conversation works.

I had qualified as an analyst a year before this and I was shocked at hearing this. Two days later I went to him for a supervision and I said to him that I had been very surprised at this remark of his. He looked at me with his owl-like eyes for what seemed at least two minutes and then he said:

Nevertheless I think that what I said is true.

For me a sign that what he said is true is that if it is really believed that a conversation 'works' – i.e. can have a healing influence on oneself and on another – then there is no need to invent spurious phrases like *clinical material*. In the two supervisions I had with Bion he said to me once or twice:

Now tell me the next part of the conversation.

Yes, so psycho-analysis is a conversation, a conversation of a particular kind and yet a conversation. What I want to examine here is the contours of this conversation.

I have entitled this lecture *The Unfocussed Stare* which phrase is borrowed from Marion Milner where she says:

I myself had learnt when writing the Joanna Field books, for instance, about having observed that there were two kinds of attention, both necessary, a wide unfocused stare, and a narrow focused penetrating kind, and that the wide kind brought remarkable changes in perception and enrichment of feeling.[1]

Both these kinds of attention are necessary. The narrow-focussed penetrating kind is to solve a problem in the natural world and makes use of the faculty of reasoning and the other, the 'wide unfocussed stare' for making a relationship. These two forms of attention are congruent with the directed and undirected thinking which she had learnt from Elton Mayo. So this is the essential difference in forms of thinking which she learnt from him: that directed thinking was in the service of scientific truths whose focus is particular aspects of the world, particularly the inanimate world, and undirected thinking was for establishing relationships. This insight is extremely important: that a certain kind of thinking is needed to establish relationships and, even the term 'thinking' does not convey the right arena in which we are concerned. Directed thinking prevents the possibility of undirected thinking. This means that scientific thinking, directed thinking, does not promote a relationship.

What Marion describes as *a wide-unfocussed stare*,[2] was called by Bion *reverie* and which Freud had called *evenly suspended attention*. Marion says that the main experiences of human life can never be apprehended by narrow-focussed analytic reasoning.[3] She therefore recommended this unfocussed, dreamy kind of attention. It is that attention of this kind produces the dream which makes sense out of nonsense. This condition of mind has been emphasized by others. In the third chapter I quoted also General Smuts who, in his book *Holism and Evolution* says that

> *The road is to be discovered, not so much by minute local inspection as by wide roaming and exploration and surveying over large districts.*[4]

David Shulman refers to it as *the relatively unfocused, even floating, receptive attentiveness, neither inward- nor outward-directed.*[5] I just mention these two thinkers outside of psycho-analysis but many writers and artists have known that this mode of mental attitude is what is required for original creative work. I mentioned at the end of the Chapter 1 the writer, David Mitchell, who said that what is required is to reach through to the core of one's being and clear away all the 'doctoring' that we have all been subjected to.[6] Marion Milner further said

> *While attending the training seminars during the blitz and the blackout, there was a phrase lurking in the back of my mind, something to do with Samuel Butler having said that a misgiving is a warning from God to be attended to as a man values his soul. Indeed I tried to keep a diary of misgivings about the theory I was trying to learn and when I came to give seminars myself I sometimes advised my students to do the same.*[7]

So this is an attitude of mind that requires a dual process: one is a clearing away of all beliefs and dictates that have taken up residence in my soul and the other is giving attention to the dreamy thoughts that flow out of the inner soul. These 'dreamy thoughts' that have taken up residence in my soul are quite different from those dictates that have been implanted in my mind during my training to be an analyst. For instance Freud's view that a neurosis is formed through an evasion of a sexual desire or Winnicott's teaching about primary maternal preoccupation or Melanie Klein's paranoid-schizoid and depressive positions. All these beliefs which have been implanted in me when training to be a psycho-analyst make the passageway to my own creative source difficult by insisting that I need to follow, rather than my own inner dispositions, the dictates of analysts of the past who have become authoritarian legislators. Montaigne emphasized greatly the need to follow the direction indicated by one's own inner soul – *rester soi-meme* – and banish the textbook.[8]

It is attention, but of this special kind, that is the instigator of the creative act. Why is it that emotional intercourse with another initiates the un-handicapping of the stunted component? We have just been emphasizing that dreaming is the product of a special kind of inner focus. When there is a harmonizing of two foci upon an unformed entity then it begins to assume a defined shape and expand. For this to happen it requires a state of mind devoid of expectation. The clinician needs to embark on his assignment with the attitude 'I am going to learn something, something new.' Any desire to mould what emerges into a preconceived system thwarts growth, thwarts the blossoming of new life; it prevents the emergence of blossoms coming from the creative core. Freud emphasized this:[9]

> *as soon as anyone deliberately concentrates his attention to a certain degree, he begins to select from the material before him; one point will be fixed in his mind with particular clearness and some other will be correspondingly disregarded, and in making this selection he will be following his expectations or inclinations. This, however, is precisely what must not be done. In making this selection, if he follows his expectations he is in danger of never finding anything but what he already knows; and if he follows his inclinations he will certainly falsify what he may perceive.*

Relationships do not just happen, they have to be brought into being just as much as a piece of music, poetry or sculpture also needs to be produced anew. It is the same phenomenon that Bion refers to as *reverie* or as Jan Christian Smuts refers to as a *wide roaming and exploration*:

> *the formulation of new viewpoints will depend not so much on masses of minute details, as on the consideration of the general principles in the light of recent advances, the collation and comparison of large masses of fact, and the survey of large areas of knowledge. The road is to be discovered, not so much by minute local inspection as by wide roaming and exploration and surveying over large districts.*[10]

Many writers, artists and musicians have referred to this state of mind. Another writer, David Shulman, in his book about Sanskrit thinking in mediaeval India says:

> *closer to our primary theme is the relatively unfocused, even floating, receptive attentiveness, neither inward- nor outward-directed, perhaps analogous*

on one level to the default awareness of a south Indian deity. Such states are conducive to sudden moments of unpredictable insight or 'realization'[11]

and Marion Milner quoting Elton Mayo, under whom she studied at Harvard, said that this wide-unfocussed attention is what was needed in order to make a relationship. Perhaps more accurately this wide-unfocussed stare is paradoxically both the fashioning of a relationship and its product.

* * *

A moment happens and what was dead and corpse-like suddenly becomes full of life and vigour. What has happened to bring this about? The active agent is this wide-unfocussed gaze, reverie or wide roaming exploration. This state which seems to be idle or passive is, on the contrary, highly active. Images float across the inner radar screen but these have been produced but by whom? An invisible agent but is this agent in me or in the other? It is in neither one nor the other but in an entity that incorporates you and me.

Two individuals are in a room. There is contact between them but they are not in relation to each other. A relation between two objects is not physical. This has been clearly expressed by Peter March:

> *If the mind were a system of physical relations between material objects then, in a sense, the mind would not be visible. Consider first the very simple relation <u>in front of</u>. Let's take the example where someone says that one of her hands is in front of the other. It is true, in a sense, that this relation between two objects is not itself visible – in the sense in which the objects themselves are visible. The relation exists, of course, but if we were asked to give the colour or the shape of the relation we would be stumped. So, granting that we do say that we can see that someone is in front of another person and granting further that most physical relations are discovered using visual information, still, since they have neither colour nor shape, they violate our intuition which suggests that everything which can be seen in the primary sense must have colour and shape.*
>
> *In another sense these relations are invisible because the relevant relata are not easily observable. One can say that it is a visible fact that one hand can be seen to be in front of the other. But the relations of mind exists as relations between neural structures of the person and objects which are not part of the person's body, hence, and since these relata are not visible to the naked eye, the relations themselves are not visible. We cannot see that one hand is in front of another if we can't see one of the hands.*
>
> *What this means is that if the mind is a system of relations then we would be unable to give its colour or its shape, nor would we be able to detect the relevant relations by sight.*[12]

So relation is not physical, not a bodily happening and we name it mental or spiritual. Mental or spiritual is negatively defined as a reality which is *not* physical, a reality that has *no* bodily features. Mental is a synonym for *relationship*.

The two people are in relation to one another. The relationship incorporates the two physical presences. The relationship is experienced in the dreamy images that pass across the inner radar screen. These images usually cross the radar screen of one of the two participants but when given expression by one it immediately coincides with the creative happening in the other. There are two levels of personal intercourse occurring. There is this image level which Rousseau called the *language of expression* and then its representation in the language of words. Rousseau makes the powerful statement:

> *By neglecting the language of expression we have lost the most forcible mode of speech.*[13]

This relationship is primary and what is secondary is its expression or representation but this requires more detailed examination. There is a particular problem that is troubling one of the two participants and this comes into the foreground if the analyst or therapist has an open-ness or receptivity to this problem. Receptivity to the issue occurs if the troubling matter is not foreign to the analyst. I have never had exactly the same problem as John or Mary or Martha but none of their problems are completely foreign to me. I have had a problem that resembles John's problem, that resembles Mary's problem, that resembles Martha's problem. Bion stressed that when there is some equivalence he feels more satisfied. This is what he says:

> *On the whole I am more satisfied with my work if I feel that I have been through these emotional experiences than I do if the session has been more agreeable. I am fortified in this belief by the conviction that has been borne in on me by the analysis of psychotic or borderline patients. I do not think such a patient will ever accept an interpretation, however correct, unless he feels that the analyst has passed through his emotional crisis as a part of the act of giving the interpretation.*[14]

In other words the troubling matter is a shared one; one that is familiar to both analyst and patient. The analyst's attachment to a theory enables him or her to avoid this painful personal experience. I shall give one example. In a consultation with a lady the image crossed my inner radar screen of a famous Australian lady aviatrix, Nancy Bird, who in her book *My God! It's a Woman*[15] describes how at the age of four she used to jump off a fence, wave her arms calling herself an *eppy plane* so she knew from a very early age that she wanted to be a pilot. So I said to this lady I was interviewing:

> *Some people know from an early age what they want to do in life*

and she replied instantly:

> *Oh this has been the bane of my life. I have never known really what I want to do in life.*

Now why did this come to me? It was because the *not knowing what to do in life* was not foreign to me. I have for forty years practised as a psycho-analyst and trained to be one for some seven years before that so for forty-seven years I have been engaged in a profession that has largely defined my life but this problem of not knowing what to do in life was a sore affliction after leaving school. I worked for a while in a wine company in the City of London; I did some tutoring for about a year in London; I went to Lisbon and functioned as an agent for products of various English companies; I sailed off to theological college and was for ten years *in the Church*; five of them in training and then five in practice in the East End of London and then cascaded out of the Church and finally settled for a career as a psycho-analyst. So the *not knowing what to do in life* was not foreign to me. This woman was with someone who knew something about not knowing which way to proceed in life. So this image of Nancy Bird's that came across the inner radar screen was the production of the relationship which embraced both myself and the lady in question.

When I do a consultation with someone that I am planning to see in an on-going way for treatment I allow a period of three hours. In the first hour I gather some practical information about the person's place in the family of origin and whether she is married or single; whether she has children and so on. The remaining time is devoted to *idleness of mind, reverie or unfocussed gaze* and it is in this domain that the *language of expression*, that Rousseau refers to, occurs. And this *language* is focussed not upon externals but upon inner failures, inner sources of diminishment. Teilhard de Chardin in his spiritual treatise *Le Milieu Divin*[16] discusses a human being's diminishments. This image produced by one and received by the other upon the inner radar screen charts the person's own diminishments. This woman's diminishment was something that I knew about from first-hand experience.

The contact is there but an inner action needs to occur so that it is seen that the inner image is the product of a relationship and when Bion refers to a conversation he means a relationship that is enabling the intercourse between the two persons. This relationship is both between one person and another and also with the subject's own self.

* * *

Why is it that to enter into a relationship this state of *reverie* or *unfocussed gaze* is required? It is because in the unfocussed gaze images come up that are personal memories from the analyst's own past but are produced by the relationship between patient and analyst. These memories are not of the factual kind; they are dream-like memories. For instance a woman saying she hated school; a clip of a film where a champagne bottle is being smashed against a boat which is just being launched; a man describing how he shot a bird in the dark; a woman pointing at the moon. They are all *glimpses*; they are not in a context. I shall give an example: A man in his thirties was emotionally crippled that prevented him from working, from making relationships. He had an eye for pretty girls and longed to have one of them as his girl-friend but they constantly rejected him. He came into a session. He said,

> *I feel completely hopeless. I had cherished a hope that I could get better, that I could be normal like other people but now I feel totally hopeless.*

I sat there knowing that there were no words that could give him a sympathy for his despair. So I sat in silence. Then an unexpected thing happened. Memory images began to pass across the screen of my mind – memories when I had felt totally hopeless, that nothing could alleviate the gloom and one particular image came across the inner screen – when I was walking down a drab London road with a case in my hand with a few paltry belongings and having no idea where I was to go. Quite uninvited this scene came before me with a fierce intensity. I let it pass before me and I watched and then two or three other scenes from the same era passed across the inner radar. I had forgotten what it was like to feel totally at a loss and without hope in the world. I said nothing but let this cinematic performance inside of me happen. These things had happened to me but now in this encounter with the young man they were alive and vivid. The silence slid on for five or ten minutes. Then he said,

> *Last week a girl I'd love to go out with turned to me and said 'Timothy I like you and would like to see you again.'*

It was the shared experience that gave him a glimmer of hope. And this was an unspoken shared experience. That there is communication between persons at this non-verbal level is certain. This confirms both the statement made by Rousseau which I quoted and also the one by Bion. It is Rousseau who said that there is a *language of expression* which is more powerful than something expressed in words and Bion said that a psychotic or borderline patient will not take in an interpretation unless he feels that the analyst has been through a similar experience in giving his interpretation. The *language of expression* is a product of the relationship.

* * *

We can ask the question why it is that a shared experience can be taken in. It is because psychotic is equivalent to alone and isolated. Psychosis *is* isolation. It is the product of a belief – a belief that this is an isolated experience that only has happened to me. This is what makes it psychotic. Once it is shared then it loses its isolation; loses it psychotic character. In popular discourse beliefs are confined to the sphere of religion but they also rule with great power in the field of science but, because beliefs are so evident in the sphere of religion, let us have a brief look at how they operate there. In certain Christian denominations it is believed that Jesus was born of a virgin; that his mother was not penetrated and inseminated through a man's penis entering her vagina and expelling semen first into the fallopian tube where it fertilizes an egg which then later, implants on the wall of her womb. The Christian belief that this did not happen to Mary, the mother of Jesus, is visualized in art with an angel confronting Mary and delivering a message, a seed, from God into her womb. Many artists, like Leonardo da Vinci, Crivelli or Fra Angelico, have painted this scene with their own characteristic imagery. Yet we all know that a foetus does not emerge into the woman's womb unless an egg, the ovum, has previously been fertilized by the semen emitted from the man's penis. This belief is an attempt to explain genius by attributing to God, a transcendent being, as being responsible for what seems to be a more-than-human endowment. How is it that the world has been blessed on occasions with people like Socrates, the Buddha, Moses, the prophet Isaiah, Jesus, Joan of Arc, Muhammad, Raphael, Michelangelo, Kant, Shakespeare, Newton, Darwin, Einstein to mention just some of the most prominent and famous? Genius has been described as someone endowed with a divine spark; the idea that God, a being from the heavens, has fertilized the minds of these great people. In the case of Jesus it is not only the fertilizing of the man's mind but his very physical conception is attributed to a beam of light from God. So a belief is a way of explaining a supreme human quality and even with evil men like Hitler or Mao-Tse-Tung their power is attributed to a diabolic charism; in other words an extreme power is attributed to an agency beyond and above the normal human processes of achievement.

I have said that such beliefs govern not only religious people and communities but also scientific research. All beliefs, religious, scientific and artistic, come from God. What an outrageous statement. Let me explain. We do not conceptualize the world as it is but how an authority has declared it to be. So the priestly author in a particular section of the Book of Genesis told us that the world was fashioned by God in seven days; well six days because on the seventh God rested as he certainly deserved to do. But each day refers to a long period of time and those who have calculated the age of the Earth according to the Book of Genesis put it at about 6,004 years. Of course we all know that the Earth is about 4.5 billion years old. The point I am making is that we (or perhaps I should say I) do not know the age of the Earth. My belief that it is 4.5 billion years old is based on what has been passed to me by astronomers and geologists and I believe what they have told me just as people in the past believed what the author of Genesis told them. My knowledge of the world is based on belief. If I had lived in the fifteenth century I knew that the Earth is the centre of the world. Then God intervened in human history. This time God was called Copernicus and he declared in 1540 that the Sun was the centre of the solar system and that our planet travelled around it in perfect circles. So, living just after Copernicus, I knew that the Sun was at the centre and our Earth and travelled around it in perfect circles but my grandson, who was born in 1620, told me I was quite wrong because an astronomer, called Johannes Kepler, had shown in the year 1609 that the Earth and all the planets travelled around the Sun in elliptical orbits. So Copernicus was God for 69 years until he was dethroned by Kepler. I now believe not according to Copernicus but according to Kepler. In a similar way the God Newton declared in 1687 the principle of gravitation and I believed this because the God Newton had declared it. Then a new God arose called Einstein who in 1915 published his work on relativity in which he refuted Newton and the God called Einstein in whom we now believe knows that gravity is not a force but a distortion of the time-space dimension.

What I am getting at is that we do not know the world as it is but we see it according to the proclamations of certain Gods. Each new God corrects the beliefs of the previous one but a new God will always appear to challenge and displace the old one. Therefore we do not know the world as it is but we base ourselves on a series of beliefs originating in the proclamations of a God. The Gods I have referred to are those whose proclamations relate to the stable rhythms within the solar system and the rhythm of the solar system within the galaxy Milky Way and the rhythm of this our galaxy in relation to the myriad galaxies that make up our universe. We may refer to these Gods as serial monotheism because at any one period of time it is *one* God whose proclamations we believe and then when that God is displaced he is supplanted by another so we call it serial monotheism but we are about now to move in a different world which we name *the human condition*.

Our understanding of the world of human beings is conditioned not by monotheism but by polytheism. There are many gods proclaiming the nature of the human world and they frequently contradict each other. I give you this quote from Mcneile Dixon:

> *Pleasure, said Epictetus, is the chief good. It is the chiefest of evils, said Antisthenes. Men, declared Rousseau, are naturally good; they are naturally bad, said Machiavelli. It is on the same evidence that distinguished people contradict each other. Virtue, proclaimed the Stoics, is sufficient for happiness. Without external goods it is not sufficient, said Aristotle.*[17]

So Epictetus, Antisthenes, Rousseau, Machiavelli, the Stoics and Aristotle were each Gods but Gods who contradicted each other. So the *distinguished people*, the Gods of Philosophy, differ profoundly from one another. And these Gods have also their believers, just as the Gods of the solar system have theirs. The difference is that, with few exceptions, all people believe what Kepler, Newton and Einstein proclaimed but as soon as we enter the portals of Philosophy there are many Gods. In the ancient world there was Socrates, Plato, Aristotle; in the mediaeval world there was Moses Maimonides, Thomas Aquinas, Averroes; in the modern era Rousseau, Descartes, Kant. It is definitely polytheism: many Gods, each with their cohort of believers and those that believe in one of these Gods are in violent opposition to the proclamations of a different God, a God whose proclamations are antagonistic to my God in whom I believe.

This diversity is also so within any one discipline of thought, whether it be History, Anthropology, Economics, Sociology or Psychology. So also within psycho-analysis Freud has his believers, Jung has his believers, Melanie Klein has her believers, Fairbairn has his believers, Heinz Kohut has his believers, Winnicott has his believers, Bion has his believers and each group of these believers follow *their* God and repudiate other Gods. The point of similarity between these philosophical or psychological Gods and those of the solar system is that in neither is the reality itself apprehended but rather what is proclaimed by the God I have bowed my head to in humble submission. It is the alarming truth that we do not see the human environment as it is. What about these Gods like Freud, Jung or Melanie Klein; did they see the human world as it is? Each one glimpsed truly one aspect of the human condition. Frequently they then generalized this and made the glimpse of one particularity into a nostrum for a much wider spectrum of the human world. Also this glimpse was a momentary vision seen through the lens of one individual. And we all attach ourselves to the vision of one of these Gods. Why? Bion said:

> *There is a hatred of having to learn from experience at all, and lack of faith in the worth of such kind of learning.*[18]

But wherefore this hatred and lack of faith in such learning? Why is it so? I wonder if we can get some purchase on this by considering the case of Kepler. He tracked the orbit of Mars and, contrary to the general belief in the God Copernicus, he discovered that Mars's orbit around the sun was not circular but elliptical but it took him six years before he dared to declare it? Why? I think it is that we are all desirous of being in a troupe, a company. There is a strong need in all of us to belong. To be entirely on my own, out of kilter with the rest of my fellows, is alarming, frightening. And yet it seems that one's own experience is unique. One person's experience is never an exact simulacrum of that of another. There is uniqueness and sharedness for every human being. We are each of us part of a reality in which we share and, at the same time, each is unique. But there is something about getting in touch with this uniqueness that is hated. Experience is this touching of what is unique. Sexual orgasm is one of the supreme delights for a human being and it is, in its essential nature, the union between two people. Isolation is orgasm's opposite and it is hated.

There is a difference between being alone and being isolated. What is it? When I am alone I am in a shared world; the features of my face as different from that of any other compatriot and yet I share with others a forehead, two eyes, two ears, a nose and a chin. I share yet I am different. The individual who is isolated is cut adrift from the shared world of which he or she is a part.

Just as my physiognomy is never quite the same as that of another so also this is so of my mental orientation. There is something shared with another and yet there is a difference. To be wholly at-one with another in everything is a denial of who I am. This is to introduce the relationship between someone and a God whom he believes in, the God being Melanie Klein or Tolstoy or Bergson. Just as my physiognomy is the same but different so also I cannot be Melanie Klein, or Winnicott or Bion. If I were then I would not have my own selfhood. I have to differ in some respects.

This brings me back to the *unfocussed stare* which creates a connection between me here and this person who is also here with me. It fashions this connection between these two persons and it is a connection which is different from the link between any other two persons. It also connects at a particular time and place and in a developmental moment which is unique. If, instead of fashioning this unique relationship I install, as a substitute, the psychological perspective of Melanie Klein or of Winnicott or of Kohut then I am, by definition, not articulating the unique relationship between myself and this person who is with me in the room but rather offering instead a generalized story of *a* relationship but not *this* relationship. Also the principles that give definition to this unique bond are not seen because they are smothered inside a concealing artefact. These principles are particular to this unique relation and yet have a wider compass of relevance because one of the two terms will be present not only in this relation which I have with Tony but <u>may</u> give a shape to my other relationships because one term in those others is the same. Also it is important to realize that a principle that becomes evident in one relationship is 'visible' because it has been created and this new creation remains a constructive force in other relationships.

* * *

There is another perspective that has a connection to the theme of this chapter. The state of *free-floating attention* or *reverie* or *unfocussed gaze* or *a wide roaming and exploration* which are all different verbal expressions for the same inner state of mind. The first three of these expressions are formulations by psycho-analysts whereas the last is by an academic and politician.[19] There is inherent in this state a purpose of discovery. It is a state that looks passive and self-contained but in fact it penetrates into the area seeking-a-solution within the partnership.

Two further aspects to this need consideration: that the person here today is not the same as the person who was here yesterday. Development or deterioration is always in process. Now this is so of the individual but it is also so of social groups. In Britain in the 1950s homosexual acts between men was a criminal offence and termed 'acts of gross indecency.' Fifty years later a sexual partnership between two men has the blessing of society and is referred to as *gay marriage*. This symptomatic change has its roots in a deep transformation of the social group. The social group is different in its orientation. Other symptom changes within the same society and within the same time period are the abolition of the death penalty, the increase in divorce and its being viewed with greater favour, the condemnation of fox hunting and the great increase in restaurants serving food from Thailand, Korea and India. So this state of mind that is being recommended can, under favourable circumstances, discover the deep currents that have given rise to these surface differences. Social groups are in a state of change and development constantly. There have been periods when a society has continued for centuries in one mode such as the Dark Ages in southern Europe or the Mandarin governance in China. There have also been times of rapid revolution and change that have taken place within twenty or thirty years.

Notes

1 Milner, Marion (1987). *The Suppressed Madness of Sane Men*. p. 81. [The Framed Gap]. London & New York: Tavistock Publications.
2 Ibid.
3 Milner, Marion (1984). *On Not Being Able to Paint*. pp. 84–85. London: Heinemann.
4 Smuts, Jan Christiaan (1926/1996). *Holism and Evolution*. p. 7. Gestalt Journal Press Inc.
 (A division of The Center of Gestalt Development – PO Box 990, Highland, New York 12528. ISBN # 0-939266-26-)
5 Shulman, David (2012). *More Than Real: A History of the Imagination in South India*. p. 141. Cambridge, MA & London: Harvard University Press.
6 David Mitchell interviewed at the New Zealand Writers' Festival. Recorded on the Book Show on 21st January 2009.
7 Milner, Marion (1987). *The Suppressed Madness of Sane Men*. p. 9. [Introduction]. London & New York: Tavistock Publications.
8 Zweig, Stefan. (2015). *Montaigne*. London: Pushkin Press.
9 Freud, S. (1912). *Recommendations to Physicians Practising Psycho-Analysis*. S.E.v.XII. pp. 111–112. London: The Hogarth Press & The Institute of Psycho-Analysis.
10 Smuts, Jan Christiaan (1926/1996). *Holism and Evolution*. p. 7. Gestalt Journal Press Inc.
11 Shulman, David (2012). *More Than Real: A History of the Imagination in South India*. p. 141. Cambridge, MA & London: Harvard University Press.
12 'The Mind as Relation' by Peter March – privately circulated.
13 Rousseau, Jean-Jacques (2013). *Emile*. p. 341. Mineola, NY: Dover Publications.
14 Bion, W.R. (1992). *Cogitations*. p. 291. London & New York: Karnac Books.
15 Bird, Nancy (1990). *My God! It's a Woman*. p. 9. Sydney: Angus & Robertson.
16 Teilhard de Chardin, Pierre (1960). *Le Milieu Divin*. pp. 58–62. London: HarperCollins.
17 Mcneile Dixon, W. (1958). *The Human Situation*. pp. 53–54. Penguin Books.
18 Bion, W.R. (1961/1968). *Experiences in Groups*. p. 89. London: Tavistock Publications.
19 The three psycho-analysts being Freud, Bion and Marion Milner and the other one being of Jan Christian Smuts.

Chapter 7

The knowledge of being

> *The conception of a noumenon, that is, of a thing which must be cogitated not as an object of sense, but as a thing in itself (solely through the pure understanding), is not self-contradictory, for we are not entitled to maintain that sensibility is the only possible mode of intuition.*[1]
>
> —Immanuel Kant

In the last chapter I focussed on the emotional state that fostered and enabled an inner connection between two persons. Such communication is the province of Art. This planet with its human, animal, plant and chemical composition is traditionally viewed through three separate lenses: Religion, Science and Art. Science examines the chemical and physical composition of any existent thing in the universe; it might be the Milky Way Galaxy, the structure of aluminium, the molecular structure of the DNA or the mode in which sedimentary rocks have been formed. So then what is Art? Art is that province of knowledge concerned with communication between human beings, between any one human being and the external world or the inner relation between an individual and his selfhood. As psycho-analysis is a particular instance of communication between human beings it is therefore an Art. It is a perpetrated falsehood when psycho-analytic events are referred to as 'Scientific Meetings.' So we have defined Science and Art but what about Religion? What is its province of knowledge? I will take you on a personal journey.

I was aged 21. I had arrived at theological college a few days before. I was sitting in a lecture hall together with 30 other students. I waited and then in came a priest; tall, long nose, sensitive eyes, very fair skin and sandy hair. As he came in we all stood up, he knelt beside the dais and said a short prayer asking for God's guidance in what he was going to teach. He spoke in a rough north-country accent. There was no doubt that whatever he was going to say, however abstract, whatever metaphysical heights he would take us to, would always be grounded in the faith of a simple man. This is what George's voice said to me at his very first utterance. Within two minutes he had abandoned his textbook, left his seat at his desk and was walking up and down the classroom in front of us, lecturing from his head as he went.

He was talking from his own soul and he did so non-stop for three quarters of an hour. In that very first lecture my heart opened to what he was revealing. There had been a yearning in me from my earliest days to understand the world in which I found myself. Now here at last I had found someone who wanted to understand the universe in the deepest way. His subject was *Ontology* – the science of Being, the mystery of Being. He gave us four lectures a week on the subject for a year. But in that very first lecture I sighed with inward relief. I had arrived home. I had found what I had been looking for all my life. Here was someone whose task was to try and grasp the mystery of the universe and convey his understanding to us, the students, who had been entrusted into his care. Yes, four lectures a week for a whole year on Being – nothing else, just Being. I was as gripped by his every word just as much as the addict is magnetized to his drug. At the end of that year a foundation had been laid in my heart and mind which has never left me. It has been a rock that has withstood the tidal waves that have blown me this way and that but never been able to shatter that rock. It had been planted too solidly into the bed of the ocean. So what did I learn and how did I learn it?

Now I want to transport you forwards to the present day, fifty years later and tell you the foundation stone of my emotional life, the rock around which the life of my mind is formed. There are two truths of which I am completely certain. The first is that there is a universe – so vast that it is beyond the capacity of our imagination to visualize it. To cross our own galaxy, just one of millions, yes, just to cross from one end to the other of our own galaxy takes 60,000 light years. Something so vast that it is incomprehensible and yet this is just one of thousands of galaxies swirling around in the vastness of space. But the size of it does not matter and I don't remember George ever elaborating on this. He had more important things to say. I do remember though him saying that it was impossible to imagine nothing, no-thing, no-being or nonbeing, as existentialist philosophers define it. I remember him saying that sometimes he woke at night and imagined going in a spacecraft to the very end of the universe and there meeting a high wall and he would climb up it and look over but there on the other side was nothing: no-thing but that he would keep seeing a shadowy something. Imagination is of something so it is a useless instrument when it comes to an absence. A favourite author in my youth was G.K. Chesterton and he understood well what George was conveying in his fable-like journey:

> *The imagination is supposed to work towards the infinite; though in that sense the infinite is the opposite of imagination. For the imagination deals with an image. And an image is in its nature a thing that has an outline and therefore a limit.*[2]

Infinite means no limit. In fact the only way the imagination deals with this is to construct a monster. We have to ask what is the absence of which this monster is the concrete representation? Imagination is a faculty through which we create and make our own the sensations that bombard our senses. But in the face of nothing, of no stimuli hitting the organism the imagination is left bereft and helpless. So my first truth is the knowledge that there is reality, there is Being; that it just is, has always been there. It just exists, cannot not exist; an existence which is permanent. I cannot shrug my shoulders and say that there is a universe but there could just as well not be. Only a little reflection tells me that the universe just is; that permanence is built into it; it could not not-be. So permanence is elemental to the character of being. It is as essential to being as extension is to any piece of matter. So that is the first truth and for me it is a marvel for which I am daily thankful. Because it is there, the basis of everything, we can fail to notice it – *it*: the most fantastic thing is that there is a world, that there is existence, that you and I are all here. It is only when we go into a desert that we notice the absence of trees. They are so much part of our landscape that we take them for granted. With Being it is more so. The fact of existence is so obvious, so unavoidable, so part of us, so basic in everything that we see it not. Macneille Dixon said it so clearly:

> *The first and fundamental wonder is existence itself. That I should be alive, conscious, a person, a part of the whole, that I should have emerged out of nothingness, that the Void should have given birth not merely to things, but to me. Among the many millions who throughout the centuries have crossed the stage of time probably not more than a handful have looked about them with astonishment, or found their own presence within the visible scene in any way surprising.*[3]

It is so fantastic that it dwarfs all our miseries, even horrors like Hiroshima, the Holocaust or the AIDS Epidemic. As Paul Tillich says it is an ultimate upon which we place all our confidence. So that is the first truth of which I am absolutely certain and which confronts my mind.

The second truth is that I, Neville, had a beginning which, in my case, was some 80 years ago, and I shall have an end within a few years, months, days or hours. This is something I know and I know it with all my being. I don't just know it as some idle fact. It is not just that I know I had a beginning and know I have an end but that it characterizes my life. Just as permanence characterizes the nature of Being so also chance characterizes my selfhood. I am but I could easily not have been. This radically differentiates me from Being which just is and could not not-be. It could not not-have-been but with me it is the opposite. I might not have been. If my parents had not had sexual intercourse on that auspicious night in early October 1936 I would not be.

So here are the two truths which have a calm conviction for me. I hold these truths with complete certainty. I am in possession of them not because anyone has told them to me. I can remember well that moment when a light shone in my mind. The moment when I saw the being of the universe in the mirror of my own soul. That is not the sort of thing that anyone can teach you. George did not teach it to me; he spoke of it and I, in a moment of wonder, suddenly grasped it. The student next to me did not. It has to be personally grasped. It is an act of inner creation.

Once seen it is never lost; it is part of my own being; it is more me than my height, age, profession or nationality. That moment of seeing occurs because the inner constituents of the mind have re-arranged themselves according to the template of universal being. It was like a laser beam that does not just light up the door but also opens it. It cannot be forgotten because my own being has been re-formed according to that reality. It, this moment of creative enlightenment, has become me just as surely as my hands are mine and in fact more surely because it is the inner principle, the essence that makes me **me**, has now been created. I can lose a hand and still be **me** but if I lose that inner essence I am no longer **me**. It is this form that fashions my knowledge and this cannot be taken from me. So, although I have passed through some severe storms on life's journey, this inner essence has remained but it is also a flexible essence, reminiscent of Aesop's fable of the Oak Tree and the Reeds. The Oak Tree boasted that it was stronger and more powerful than these diminutive reeds but then a hurricane came and blew for all its worth and the old Oak Tree was uprooted and tumbled to its end; the Reeds though bent with the wind and remained living and undaunted. It is a paradox that what is most strong and enduring in the mind is also that which is most flexible: most open to the thinking and outlook of others. I am always troubled when psycho-analysts believe they possess the truth and look with contempt upon practitioners of CBT, yoga or hydrotherapy and believe they know best. There is no system which possesses all knowledge; all we can ever do is grope towards – towards what Kant called the *noumenon*. I was struck by an incident in the Buddha's life when Upali, a follower of Mahavira, came to argue with Gotama. After a time he was convinced that the Buddha's teaching and not that of Mahavira was right. Upali decided to follow the Buddha's way but the Buddha requested him to continue to respect and support his old religious teachers as he used to.[4]

And yet there is a paradox. Out of that knowledge of being comes some tributaries flowing from it. One such tributary which is, at the same time, part of it is permanence; another is that it is single; it is one. There cannot be two. Being is one. This was well understood by Parmenides, the Greek philosopher who lived earlier than Socrates and Plato. Parmenides grasped the reality of being and that it was one and, his logic told him, unchanging and yet when he opened his eyes and saw flowers blooming, birds flying, seasons changing he said all this change must be an illusion. His inner insight told him that being was one and unchanging so what his senses told him must be an illusion. It is worth reflecting that Parmenides trusted more that inner light of understanding than what appeared to him through his senses. It is the complete reverse with modern philosophy, since the days of Locke and Descartes. This modern temper underlies the thinking of psycho-analysis, of nearly all psychiatry and psychology and the human sciences generally. Of course we know, we sophisticates, that Parmenides was wrong – he trusted his inner intuitive faculty but not what his senses told him – yet we moderns are at fault because we dismiss that inner light and believe our only pathway to knowledge is through what our senses tell us. That giant among thinkers, Thomas Aquinas, knew that the only knowledge that we could put our trust in is what comes to us through that intuitive faculty *together with* the registration of sense impressions. We moderns, we, the progeny of a vast folly, are in a worse state than Parmenides because he saw, heard and smelt the changing world around him and named it an illusion so he did not not-see it but named it an illusion but we moderns don't say that the intuitive understanding of being is an illusion; we just say that it does not exist. We wipe it away, pretend that there is nothing to explain. Parmenides was wiser than ourselves. How far have we come in 2,500 years? Oh yes, aeroplanes, television and nuclear bombs but . . . are we more advanced or have we deteriorated? That wise thinker, Michael Polanyi, put it thus:

> *A powerful movement of critical thought has been at work to eliminate any quest for an understanding that carries with it the metaphysical implications of a groping for reality behind a screen of appearances. . . . Our acknowledgment of understanding as a valid form of knowing will go a long way towards liberating our minds from this violent and inefficient despotism.*[5]

This is the moment to emphasize that there are two pathways to knowledge. First there is knowledge of the world that we take in through the senses. We are passive in the face of the sound, colour and touch of things around us. When I use the term 'passive' maybe the better word would be 'receptive' because there is active consent to the inflow of information from the senses. This is one pathway to knowledge. The other is through a faculty which actively grasps Being itself but does not have knowledge of any particular whether it be a star, a pelican flying overhead or a dream. It is a faculty that does not register variety; it is blind to colour, deaf to sound, anaesthetized to feeling. It grasps just one thing: being, just being. Without this I cannot know when I look at you, the reader, whether you are real or whether I am hallucinating you. You might all be dream figures were it not for this faculty of the real. You might ask how these two connect? There are two pathways giving two forms of knowledge: one is through the senses that impresses particular aspects of the environment upon the mind. The other is the mind in action which grasps reality itself. Freud addressed this issue in his paper *Two Principles of Mental Functioning*. He starts by saying that what the mind primarily wants is pleasure. This is the primitive occurrence that is happening in the mind but then, he says,

> *the psychical apparatus had to decide to form a conception of the real circumstances in the external world and to endeavour to make a real alteration in them. A new principle of mental functioning was thus introduced; what was presented in the mind was no longer what was agreeable but what was real, even if it happened to be disagreeable. This setting up of the reality principle proved to be a momentous step.*[6]

Freud then went on to say that the sense organs are now directed towards the external world whereas before the focus of the psychical apparatus was upon the internal pleasure which the organism derived from the sensations which came to it. At first sight it may look as though what I am proposing is not much different from what Freud is saying. We are both claiming that the ego, or the psychical apparatus as the translators, render it for us, actively engages with the environment. The difference though is this: that for Freud the source of this action is located in the sense organs which are actively geared to the environment in its particular varieties but the position that I am taking is that what is occurring is an act of mind that grasps reality, a reality that is devoid of any sensory qualities. So there is the knowledge which comes from a receptivity to the variety of sensory qualities in the environment and then the act of mind that grasps reality devoid of any sensory quality but what is it that connects them? I do not know the answer to this but I do know that there is a something that connects them and does so with certainty. As an analogy I have often used the story of how Helen Keller who, though blind and deaf, came to understand how words represented things in the world. Her Teacher, as she called Mary Ann Sullivan, put her right hand under a tap and poured water onto it and into the left hand she spelt the letters W-A-T-E-R and suddenly in a flash Helen realized that these strange scratchings on her left hand represented that cold fluid flowing onto her right hand. What was that something that joined these two? So, also, I look and see you, the reader, through my eyes and through the faculty of being, I grasp being itself. These are two pathways to knowledge: one grasps the real but no change or variety and the other gives me change and variety and then this mysterious something joins the two up so that I am quite certain that you, the reader, are all really there and not just a figment of my imagination. There is a word that has been used to describe this mysterious something but I prefer not to use it. Often when we once name something we do so only for the sake of packaging it away into some inner filing cabinet and believe then that we know what it is. I think often that naming is a screen for ignorance. A little known author, Christopher Burney, said at the end of a remarkable little book:

> *I have no objection to people inventing all the words they need. All the fun in talking and speculation comes from seeing whether you can fit words in to fill gaps in your knowledge. But people get into bad habits. They turn words into things; they pretend they're sticks and beat people with them; and when a word has acquired enough status it actually has the power to hurt.*[7]

And it can hurt us by deceiving us into thinking that we understand something because we have named it. So let us leave that connecting something without any word but I want you to remember Helen Keller and her remarkable Teacher, Mary Ann Sullivan.

So I have this knowledge that my own being, my own selfhood had a beginning and has an end and this is the foundation of my knowledge and experience and yet . . . there is only one being, one universe so I must be part of it. There are two contradictories that confront me: I am limited, I am finite, a mere accident of chance, a fragment that came into being and then will perish and yet . . . there is only one being and it can never not have been. That is what is meant by *permanence*. There must be, it seems, some seed of eternity within my selfhood. How can this contradiction be reconciled? I must now turn to something which has been preserved within all great religious traditions: mystery. But before I elaborate upon it I want to emphasize that I owe myself as an accident of chance to the fact that there is a universe that existed before me and that, in some mysterious way, must be my mother and that therefore my existence is a totally unmerited gift. I have no rights. I cannot carry a banner and say 'I have a right to exist' – all I can do is to be profoundly thankful for the fact of my existence, the fact that I came to be. Again I will quote my dear Chesterton:

> *A whole generation has been taught to talk nonsense at the top of its voice about having 'a right to life' and 'a right to experience' and 'a right to happiness.*[8]

My good friend, Bob Gosling who used to be Chairman at the Tavistock Clinic when I worked there and who later became a trusted friend wrote in a letter to me two years before he died the following:

> *In my view what gave me life, or at least saved me from death, is the amazing fact that my mother had inborn tendencies to minister to my infant helplessness and that they were sufficiently supported socially and culturally for her to work the miracle. From my point of view this was a totally unmerited gift – Grace, in fact. Ave Maria! So the choices we have to make every day now in so far as they are very derived or developed forms of this first relationship depend on how much we can acknowledge and honour this Gift (and become identified with it).*

I stress this because this 'nonsense' that Chesterton refers to – i.e. that view that I have a right to be happy – pervades the world of psychotherapy like a plague bacillus. I will return now to 'mystery.'

Religious people are often justly accused of importing God or something from the spirit world to explain things which are enigmatic but which, with effort, have been or can be explained by science. The phrase *deus ex machina* is used to describe this sleight of hand. But there is a fault, just as bad, on the side of scientists and philosophers: attempting to explain something which is beyond the capability of the human mind to grasp. Our minds, as Kant emphasized, are limited in their capacity. The mind's competence has grown with increased brain size from the time of *homo erectus* some three million years ago to *homo sapiens* of today and, if we have not blown ourselves up before then, our descendants in three million years of time may be able to grasp with their minds what we cannot manage today. The religious word 'mystery' refers to this limitation of mind. We see this very clearly when there are two matters which are both true and yet seem to be contradictories; they are both true but our minds cannot reconcile them. When scientists and philosophers try to do so they are refusing to acknowledge the mind's limitation. Their antagonism to religion makes them refuse to consider even the meaning of 'mystery.'

So these are the two pieces of certain knowledge that I have: that the universe is permanent, eternal and without limit and yet me, as part of it, is limited and these two truths seem to contradict each other; such a contradiction was called by the philosopher Kant an antinomy. I cannot understand how these two can co-exist but rather than submit to the arrogance of the solution installed in Christian theology or the opposite solution of Spinoza I prefer to say it is a mystery. They are both true but it is beyond my comprehension to know how these two truths can be reconciled. It is not only me who cannot grasp it but even minds as great as Saint Augustine or Spinoza.

* * *

Has what I am saying anything to do with psychotherapy? Anything to do with the healing of the mind? Please be patient because now I am going to transport you back again to fifty years ago when I was listening to George in that cheerless lecture hall. How was it that what he said implanted itself so deeply within my soul, into the very core of my being? I believe it was because it was deeply ingrained in his own mind and heart. From my bedroom which overlooked a pathway surrounding the buildings I would occasionally see George walking energetically up and down for five or ten minutes. I felt sure that he had suddenly understood something and was breathing it into his mind. Because it was deeply ingrained into the core of his mind he was able to transmit it into mine; and transmit it in such a way that it became a piece of knowledge which, like a template, organized my own mind into a pattern around it. The act of understanding in which I grasped being was entirely my own. It was a personal act and yet . . . it had been transmitted, created in fact, by George's mind. Here again is a contradiction: entirely my own personal act and yet . . . created by another. I won't quite call that mystery because I think it can be explained but not without opening our minds to ontological reflection. It was not the words that he spoke but rather his personal mind which was the effective agent. He was therefore a psychotherapist, an amazingly effective psychotherapist. I have since that time had the good fortune to encounter others who are psychotherapists though they would never puff themselves up with such a term. 'Healing someone else's psyche?' they would say. 'Oh no I have only ever been able to heal myself and even that I have not managed very well.' It is only those arrogant professionals, like myself, who dare to call ourselves psychotherapists. So through George's agency I implanted something into my heart which has remained a foundation inside myself and, I believe, will remain so until the end of my life.

An act of understanding is something which transports knowledge from the outside, from the surface, right into the heart of the mind. This is why understanding takes much longer than knowing something. Basil Hume, the cardinal in England for the last two decades of the twentieth century, who taught me French literature when I was at school, said:

> *you know more than you understand. Understanding comes slowly, trailing behind knowledge.*[9]

I cannot understand something *for* someone. That great Russian thinker, Vladimir Soloviev, said you cannot make someone understand something. My first job as a psychotherapist then is to trust the knowledge which is deeply in me. To do this I need to distinguish between stuff that lies on the surface and that which is in the mind's centre. When I read something new which has gripped me I am always reluctant to pass it on to others. First I want to edit it, take possession of it, relate it to other truths so my own being becomes altered by it. I know something but I want to believe what I know. When I heard George, I had an act of understanding but I did not believe it. My whole life has been a process of believing what I knew and that inner task it has taken me fifty years to achieve.

I think I must have known what George was speaking of in those lectures before he spoke them. I believe that very young children grasp great metaphysical truths that adults often miss. Since being in Australia I have corresponded regularly with Isca Wittenberg, a well-known psychotherapist who worked for many years at the Tavistock Clinic with children and adolescents. In a letter seventeen years ago, in response to a paper I had sent her about reverence, she wrote this to me:

> *My feeling is that dependence does include fear as well as love but reverence implies an awareness of goodness which starts at the baby's wonder at mother's goodness. . . . I believe that the baby looking at a few months at mother adoringly is aware that she contains something that is both hers but also not hers – an endowment which has been given.*

Our journey is to first find and then believe the truths that we have found. After all, if the universe is eternal, without cause and I am part of it then it must be in me. It is this which has been deeply in me since my birth (and even during my nine months as a foetus) that I have to find. This is my prime work as a psychotherapist. I doubt very much whether this can be achieved without some form of meditation or reflection.

The goal of reflection or meditation is contemplation; reflection is like foreplay before the sexual act. The object of contemplation is Being but not Being, the infinite and eternal, outside of myself but as the 'ground of my being' as Tillich put it. As nothing is excluded from being then the whole universe with myself in it is the object of a gaze of wonder. This marvel gathers me into itself. The difference between madness and sanity is this: that in madness I become possessed by a sensual object; in sanity I am possessed by the infinite which is not sensual but is what makes the sensual real. This is for me an important perspective: that when I am mad, when I am possessed by a fragment of the universe. I have allowed a part rather than the whole to take possession of me. When I am sane I have allowed the infinite to take possession of me.

So I believe that I grasped Being because George had grasped it in his own heart. Because it was a personal possession for him, or, more accurately, he was personally possessed by it so I was able to grasp it. We had, at the time, another philosopher, Martin, who taught us epistemology. He taught it because he had been ordered to teach it. It was not something that consumed his soul. I am sure that had he taught us Ontology I should never have had that groundbreaking insight that came to me when listening to George. To the end of my life I shall be grateful to George and to this day I feel a love for him. I cannot feel this about Martin. This difference that I am talking about is what determines the effectiveness of a psychotherapist. Please do not be deceived. Don't come to me with the psychotherapist's curriculum vitae. He may have trained at one of the best psycho-analytic institutes, he may have been schooled at the Menninger Clinic, Chestnut Lodge or the Tavistock; he may have a Ph.D. in Psychotherapy. He may have read many a learnt book. He may have written many books (!). This tells you nothing. Passions of the soul are not guaranteed by any of these impressive labels. I will quote to you from Paul Tillich:

> *Look at the student who knows the content of the hundred most important books of world history, and yet whose spiritual life remains as shallow as it ever was, or perhaps becomes even more superficial. And then look at an uneducated worker who performs a mechanical task day by day, but who suddenly asks himself: 'What does it mean, that I do this work? What does it mean for my life? What is the meaning of my life?' Because he asks these questions, that man is on the way into depth, whereas the other man, the student of history, dwells on the surface among petrified bodies, brought out of the depth by some spiritual earthquake of the past. The simple worker may grasp truth, even though he cannot answer his questions; the learned scholar may possess no truth, even though he knows all the truths of the past.*[10]

I believe that we suffer in our present age from a very serious disease. It is called 'professionalization.' The signs of it are a language only used by this élite, a methodology that becomes a cult and assessment based on the number of things done or attended. We have come to believe that if we have a certificate detailing all these impressive achievements, then we know. Give me every time the 'simple worker' that Tillich refers to rather than this highly acclaimed professional. There are strengths and weaknesses in every age; there are neuroses that engulf whole epochs. We are all familiar with the *folie à deux* but Erich Fromm reminds us that there is also *folie à millions*.[11] So a strength of our era is scientific rigour but a weakness is the over-valuation of diplomas, degrees and certificates and valuation based on external performances. An individual can have achieved great acclaim in the academic world and yet be ignorant. William Hazlitt says:

> *You will hear more good things on the outside of a stage-coach from London to Oxford, than if you were to pass a twelvemonth with the undergraduates, or heads of colleges, of that famous university; and more home truths are to be learnt from listening to a noisy debate in an ale-house, than from attending to a formal one in the House of Commons.*[12]

So the truth that I am trying to emphasize is this: that to be possessed by the infinite, the ultimate, is sanity but to be possessed by a fragment of the whole, by a sensual piece of the whole, is madness. This is because the infinite is in all the sinews of my being whereas the fragment, the sensual bit, shuts out some functions of my personality. Madness is the destruction of essential parts of me which then become replaced with hallucinations and delusions. But then the matter goes further than that. It is that the ultimate of which I am possessed is also present in my patient, in my client, in my colleague, in you, the reader. My problem is to reach this inside of myself. The job of the psychotherapist is to make contact with the infinite within himself. When he speaks from this then his patient also has the possibility of finding the root of sanity within himself.

Summary

So the psychotherapist needs to become the possession of Being, Absolute Being. As Being penetrates all the variety of everything so also his own self is interpenetrated by Being, Absolute Being. That is the first essential. That is the first step. Human beings are unable *not* to make the Absolute. If they do not create the Being that is there they create a fragment of the whole into Absolute Being. If this is done then we have fanaticism in one of its many forms: Communism, Catholicism, Islam, Judaism, Buddhism, Hinduism, Freemasonry, Psycho-analysis, Self-Psychology, Klein theory, Psychology, Sociology, Economics, Determinism, Science, Progress, the Aesthetic, the Moral, Australia, England, America, Japan or any other nation, tribe or ideology on the earth.

The second principle is that I perceive the world according to the way my own being is constituted. I shall then see this individual that I am talking to in the light of Being which also penetrates his or her unique individuality *as he or she is*. If, on the other hand, I have made the fragment absolute then I will persuade myself that this is right and I will impose it upon my patient. I first persuade myself of the truth of this fragment and then I impose it upon the other.

So the act of seeing has a power. It is like the laser beam which not only lights up the door but opens it. If I can be myself, totally myself, then the other has the possibility of being totally himself or herself. For me to be myself and for you, whoever you are, to be yourselves – this is the aim of psychotherapy.

Notes

1 Kant, Immanuel (1978). *Critique of Pure Reason*. p. 188. Everyman Library. J.M. Dent & Sons.
2 Chesterton, G.K. (1938). *Autobiography*. p. 107. London: Hutchinson & Co.
3 Mcneile Dixon, W. (1958). *The Human Situation*. pp. 72–73. Penguin Books.
4 Rahula, Walpola (1985). *What the Buddha Taught*. p. 4. London & Bedford: Gordon Fraser.
5 Polanyi, Michael (1959). *The Study of Man*. pp. 20–21. Chicago, IL: University of Chicago Press.
6 Freud, Sigmund (1911). *Formulations on the Two Principles of Mental Functioning*. p. 219. S.E.XII. London: The Hogarth Press & The Institute of Psychoanalysis.
7 Burney, C. (1962). *Descent from Ararat*. p. 36. London: Macmillan and Co.
8 Chesterton, G.K. (1938). *Autobiography*. p. 335. London: Hutchinson & Co.
9 Hume, George Basil (1979). *Searching for God*. p. 35. London, Sydney, Auckland & Toronto: Hodder & Stoughton.
10 Tillich, Paul (1964). *The Shaking of the Foundations*. pp. 61–62. Penguin Books.
11 Fromm, Erich (1972). *Psychoanalysis and Religion*. p. 16. Bantam Books.
12 Hazlitt, William (1908). The Ignorance of the Learned. In *Table Talk or Original Essays*. p. 75. Everyman Library No 321. London & Toronto: J.M. Dent & Sons.

Chapter 8

Creative intercourse between analyst and patient, between mother and child, between teacher and student

> *We communicate truth not by verbal or non-verbal signs but by an interior experience of a sharing of minds.*[1]
> —St. Augustine

We return now to the crucial question: what is required of the clinician for the handicapped function to begin to grow and become unhandicapped? The answer is that if he speaks from his own personal core this has a generative effect upon the undeveloped function both in himself and in the patient. I give first an example:

> A woman aged 35, whom I shall call Emily, had a wish to meet a decent man and have a child. She had endured ten years of psycho-analytic psychotherapy four days a week and this had so far not eventuated in her desired outcome. I met with her and we arranged that she would start therapy once a week. (I say 'therapy' though, by my definition, it was psycho-analysis. It is a mistake to define psycho-analysis by number of times a week or length of sessions). After two-and-a-half years of analysis she linked up with a boyfriend, they became lovers and she then became pregnant and gave birth to a baby girl. The birth was in June 2014 when I was in Israel. One day, while she was pregnant, she said she knew that this favourable outcome had come about through the current treatment process.
> *What was it about the therapy that produced this result, do you think?* I asked her.
> *I don't know if you realize,* she said to me, *but in the time you have been seeing me, you have never said anything which you yourself don't really think.*

I said in the last chapter that in those lectures on Ontology delivered to me by George that the reason why they had such an impact upon me was that he spoke from his own soul and it was this same phenomenon that had so powerful an effect on Emily; that generative communication occurs not at the level of representative language but at the preverbal, soul to soul, contact between the two persons. This implies that this is so because the two souls share in a union of which both are participants. And when in the last chapter I referred to those images that emerge on the inner radar screen these have been produced by the creative union enjoyed by the two persons.

We have stressed that when the handicapped function is seen and attended to, this in itself is already a sign that healthy development is on its way. It means that there is a knowledge of the wholesome state and entirety of each participant and that, in the light of this, there is some deficiency that is interfering with the full-blooded intercourse that should be occurring. This is because something dysfunctional cannot be seen except from the perspective of something that is functioning, or on the way to be functioning, in a satisfactory way. It is that the unhealthy is being seen through the eyes of a healthy one. Differentiation of one thing from another is through contrast. We are familiar with such contrasts: good and bad, healthy and unhealthy; the dark is only seen when silhouetted against the light. So when the dysfunctional element is seen it tells us that a healthy operation is already becoming established. Clinically it is very important that this be focussed upon, attended to, rather than the dysfunctional element which is now visible. Why is this?

Attention is a generative force because it flows from the united core of the two persons. Attention to something is not a detached transaction but rather it is an engine with power. So if the dysfunctional element is the focus of attention then this element grows and expands. Attention is a force that grows and expands the object focussed upon. One can think of it, from a different perspective, in Bion's terms, as a waking-dream. The dreaming is like a maternal breast that is nurturing the feature that is thwarted. The clinician's task therefore is to be a maternal nurse to the newborn child or like a gardener who waters the sprouting seed. This requires the clinician to infer the shape and contours seen by an observer who has recognized the dysfunction. The temptation is to make declarations about the dysfunctional component. Even if declarations are made about how destructive or demoralizing is the dysfunctional element it brings the focus of attention upon it and this leads to expansion and growth. What needs attention is the seer and not the handicapped component that is seen. This requires a decoding by the clinician because it is not what is seen but this newly won capacity to see that requires growth and development. How has this new vision come to be? Careful thought and restrained inference are needed so that the principle of this new development expands and grows. Inference and not sight is the developmental instrument.

This attentive inference is a creative agent but, as is so with every function, it is composed of several factors. Notation is one and Attention is another. Notation and Attention are the third and fourth items on the horizontal axis of Bion's grid. First the thing or event is noted. This may be an external matter like I look out of the window and see that it is raining or it may be an internal happening. I am looking at a clock on my desk and there floats into my mind a large clock that was in my dream last night. But it is this **I** that is the creative factor. This is composed of several performers one of which is notation. So the two examples just given, one external and one internal, are events which have been noted. This notation shades into attention when the observed happening is selected out from the surrounding occurrences for a specific focus. If we follow Bion then comes Column Five which he entitled *Inquiry*. The inference from what he says is that this should not be pursued with obstinacy. Marion Milner also indicated that a narrow-focussed kind of attention misses out on the vital experiences of living.[2] I made reference in the introduction to ostensible illusions. These are illusions that have a definite shape, a distinct form. I gave examples such as I believe I am dead, I believe that I do not exist, I believe that when I die that the rest of the universe will come to an end. So the word ostensible means we are referring to a belief that has a definite form. This can be a visible image such as the sight of my mother entering my room though she died twenty years ago. It can be an audible illusion such as when I hear a voice telling me that I am hated. So these are visible and audible illusions but an ostensible illusion may have no visible or auditory properties but consist in a belief about the form in which my existence presents itself to me.

So, to take as an example, the belief that I am dead. How does this come about? All illusions come into being through a *magical act*. This act is composed of two components: one negative and the other positive. In the negative component the act obliterates the reality that is there. In this case it is the evidence of my being alive. What happens is that the impulse for coherence takes over. What is noticeable is that illusions are always unitary; they obey the *lust for coherence*. I do not have an illusion that I am alive but a realization that there may be some part of me that is dead. This kind of assessment indicates that we are in touch with reality rather than an illusion; this is because in the realization there is knowledge that it is not the whole of me that is dead but just a part. Illusions are always a totality. It is never partly this and partly that. In illusions there are no qualifications. Reality however is always a composite of different and frequently contradictory elements. So the thrust for coherence takes hold of one element and makes it all-embracing, makes it the totality. In this case there is an aspect of me that is dead. Let us say, for instance, that someone starts talking to me about probability theory within statistics. I am not interested in this. It does not enliven me; the unfortunate interlocutor is talking to a corpse. The thrust for coherence grabs hold of this one aspect and makes it total. Now I believe that I am dead. So the illusion changes what is a metaphor into concrete fact, changes the partial into a totality. Illusions are never metaphorical. When I say I am dead to probability theory in statistics the word 'dead' is a metaphor. It is the taking of a material physical fact as an analogy for a mental reality. All mental states rely on such analogies for their description and there is a similitude between the physical state and the mental which allows for the creation of the metaphor but the illusion does not know of such concepts as similitude. Something either is or is not; one thing can never be like another. It either is another or it is not.

What has not been elucidated here is why the individual takes hold of an aspect of himself and makes of it a totality, a concrete whole. What is the situation that gives rise to this happening? It happens because of an inability to construct the real. We probably have the idea that to perceive the real is natural, is easy but this is a mistake. We live in a world where the comprehension of our surroundings is governed by illusions. Illusions are ingested; reality is created.

So the implication is that it is easier to attach to an illusion than to apprehend the real. In Chapter 5, I quoted Bernard Berenson, the great art critic, and with a risk of boring you I will quote to you again what he says:

> *the most difficult thing in the world is to see clearly and with one's own eyes, naïvely. . . . Only when a person is to become an artist is a systematic effort made to teach him. But note how it is done. . . . He was set to copy simple drawings of his own master, or of other artists. Then the antique was put before him, and he had to copy that. By this time his habits of vision were well on the way to becoming fixed, and, unless he were endowed with unusual powers of reacting against teaching, he passed the rest of his life seeing in objects only those shapes and forms that the drawings and antiques put before him had pointed out to him. . . . And, unless years devoted to the study of all schools of art have taught us to see with our own eyes, we soon fall into the habit of moulding whatever we look at into the forms borrowed from the one art with which we are acquainted.*[3]

What this statement of Bernard Berenson shows is that it was easier for those renaissance artists to follow an instruction from a teacher in authority than to see for themselves. This is because illusions have coherence but this is never so of reality. Reality is always a mixture. Seeing what is there requires of me an emotional creative act and, strange to say, it is the creative act that opens the mind to contradictions, to dissonance. For this to happen it has to come from my own centre. I have to produce something from my own heart in order to see what is there and my own centre is also composed of disparate and inconsistent elements. The work of apprehending this is arduous. It is a lonely work. I do it on my own. I am in collaboration with others yet not under the direction of a higher power. Great teachers have not been people who have a knowledge which they are now going to impart. The great teacher is 'learning on the job.' When Kant was lecturing he was investigating something for himself. He just had a few notes on a sheet of paper and his mind travelled along in this quest. The audience was listening to his personal quest.

This personal quest comes from the creative centre of the personality and this centre is a shared entity. There is a communicative unity in human beings. Communication would not be possible unless we were all in a unitary medium, fish in the same water. I will give an example.

> *A man, on business came once in six weeks to the city where my patient, a woman of 34 was living. He and she had sex together. She was single and wanted to marry and have children; he was married with two children aged twelve and fourteen. He said to her that when his two children were grown up he would divorce his wife and marry her. I had a somewhat cynical attitude*

towards this man. I thought, to begin with, that he might be promising this but in eight years' time when his children had become adults who knows what he would do. No one can say what he is going to feel at a future date. Feelings are registrations of realities that are present here and now. I also thought that, by holding my patient in this controlled embrace, that he was prejudicing her chance of meeting another man and having a fruitful union that would hopefully result in the children which she desired. I thought this man was ruining her chances. Now, I want to emphasize, that I did not say this to her but I thought it and I am sure that this inner thinking of mine conditioned the way I spoke with her; not only the content but the tone in which I conveyed my thoughts. Then a surprising thing happened. I woke one morning and had this startling thought:

> She is quite free to live like this. It does not sound to me very satisfactory but, after all, why do I think my life is so wonderfully satisfactory.

> I did not rush into my consulting-room and say to her 'I have had the most surprising thought: that you are quite free to carry on with this once-in-six-week sexual affair.' But I am sure this striking thought conditioned the way I related to her, both the content and the tone. I doubt if an observer would have noticed anything different in the way I engaged with her but that there was a subtle difference I am sure. The next time her lover came to town she had the most furious row with him and told him that she never wanted to see him again and she didn't. Some months later she met a man, they became lovers, they married, she had two children and lived happily ever after! Now the point I want to emphasize is this: that when I had that surprising thought it was not something produced by me, by me alone, by me in isolation. It was generated by her and me in a unified embrace, in orgasmic unity. And this inner force drove a new pathway in her outer relationships. It changed me also.

I give this example in order to emphasize that the surprising thought I had was personal and came from my centre and yet there was communication between my centre and the centre of this patient. Was it my thought or her thought? Sexual intercourse where there is bodily inter-penetration between the man and the woman represents an emotional intercourse between the man and the woman, the mother and her baby, two close friends. This union between the two, whichever two, is, like in the case just quoted, instantiated in the thought that I had, but the thought is produced by an underlying 'something.' What is this something? I give a quote from Tolstoy's *War and Peace* in order to start elucidating it. It is his description of the manner of attention in Kutuzov, the supreme commander of the Russian army in the Battle of Borodino:

> He listened to the dispatches that were brought to him, and gave directions when his subordinates demanded that of him; but when listening to the

> *dispatches he did not seem to be interested in the import of the words spoken but rather in something else – in the expression of the face and the tone of voice of those who were reporting. Long experience in war had taught him, and the wisdom of age had made him realize, that it was impossible for one man to direct hundreds of thousands of others waging a struggle with death, and he knew the outcome of a battle is determined not by the dispositions of the commander-in-chief, not the place where the troops are stationed, nor the number of cannon or the multitude of the slain, but by that intangible force called the spirit of the army, and he kept an eye on that force and guided it as far as lay within his power. Kutuzov's general expression was one of concentrated, quiet attention.*[4]

I suspect this *concentrated quiet attention* was another way of expressing *reverie* or *unfocussed gaze*. For Kutuzov this *something* was indicated by facial expression and tone of voice but what this indicated for him was what Tolstoy called *that intangible force called the spirit of the army*. This *something* is an inner spirit that animates a group and which becomes manifest in facial expression and tone of voice. So this something is what Tolstoy speaks of in another context of a *life force*. This may be full of energy and vigour or dull, diseased or dead. Wilfred Bion said that when a thought comes to an individual within a group that this thought is shared by the other members of the group. When the possessor of the thought gives it voice he finds that this is echoed in the other members of the group. So the thought is the manifestation of the spirit of the group. There is this strange paradox that what is most personal is, at the same time, a production and exposure of the group spirit; so what is *personal* is not the equivalent of an attitude that is private but a manifestation of the group within the individual but the group existing in a concentrated unity. What is personal is the accurate insight of one individual into this *intangible force* that animates the group. So he is not voicing a thought that is private to him but one whose spirit is active in the group.

It is apposite to clarify what appears to be a contradiction: that something is a lonely work yet, at the same time, it is done in collaboration with others. It is necessary first to realize that ninety-nine percent of our knowledge has come to us from our forebears. Almost all I know has been passed on to me first from my parents, who taught me to speak but then through teachers at school where I learnt mathematics, history, geography, science. You will have gathered from the last chapter that at college I learnt the history and development of religious thinking down the centuries. Then at university I learnt about psychology and in my psycho-analytic training I imbibed the teachings of Freud and his followers. And I live in a community of others who have also learnt through the same communal procedures. So I am in collaboration with others but, at the same time, there is something that I do on my own. What is it? To answer it requires us to realize that all this imported knowledge through educational institutions concerns the *expression* of what I see, *expression* of what I know. A teacher is a midwife who brings to birth knowledge that is there; what is hidden becomes revealed. I see and then need to make manifest what I see. I have not truly seen it until I have made it manifest. Seeing and expressing are aspects of a continuum. The act of seeing is the first and fundamental step; the second one is the *expressing* of what I see but without the latter the former is not established. It is only of value when it can be seen by others but I cannot make you see. I can express what I see and this may fire the seeing in another. It does not cause the seeing in another but stimulates the desire. But I also make manifest to myself what I see. To do this I translate what I see into symbols. I say symbols rather than language because there is an imagery for what I see that precedes language. Language is the filing cabinet for a range of different images. To know the difference between imagery and language it is necessary to understand the way intellect and emotion diverge from one another. The **word** *sad* is the experience of sadness divested of the actual occurrence. The **word** points to the experience; it is not itself the experience. What we refer to as *intellect* is the assemblage of words pointing to an experience; the emotional is the experience itself. A picture, a story captures the emotion; the intellect points to it.

As I said a few minutes ago an illusion has coherence, a unifying sense, which is satisfying to the mind but reality is always a mixture; it is not coherent. There is something unsatisfying about incoherence which is why we attach ourselves to illusions which we imbibe. What is it that undoes such an illusion? When an illusion comes into contact with someone governed by the real, the illusion collapses. It does not just collapse in a moment. It takes time; there is a slow erosion of the illusion. When the illusion collapses it can be very disturbing to the patient. The patient has held onto it and it has functioned as a guiding light. Now this has collapsed and the individual is thrown to the wolves. What I mean is that no inner guide has, as yet, come into being so the individual becomes the dupe of circumstance. Whereas he had been guided by the illusion now he is now governed by the advice or directives of another. A man who had been in the thrall of an illusion that the sun set in the evening and rose in the morning by his say-so and now this illusion evaporated. He was now a helpless creature carried by the power of uncontrolled desire. This desire may be sexual, acquisitive or demanding. A sexy woman who saw a chance of appropriating for herself a sizeable portion of her lover's money lured him through sexual allurement into her power. Stripped of the magical illusion he was helpless in her power. So the illusion sometimes has the role of protecting someone from the force of another.

Nearly all psycho-analytic theories are illusions. They are generated by the *magical act* which is governed by the *lust for coherence* and so, as with all illusions, are composed first of the negative obliteration of reality as it is and then the positive construction of the illusion. Because illusions are systems they inherently shut out the reality with all its variety. Visualize this statement which I quoted in the Introduction; it comes from Isaiah Berlin; I will quote it again:

> *Systems are mere prisons of the spirit, and they lead not only to distortion in the sphere of knowledge, but to the erection of monstrous bureaucratic machines, built in accordance with the rules that ignore the teeming variety*

> *of the world, the untidy and asymmetrical inner lives of men, and crush the*
> *into conformity for the sake of some ideological chimera unrelated to the*
> *union of spirit and flesh that constitutes the real world.*[5]

Berlin indicates precisely the negative component of an illusion: that it ignores *the teaming variety of the world, the untidy and asymmetrical inner lives of men.* Our psycho-analytic theories are all illusions. If we grasp them strongly and believe them to be *the* truth then we blind ourselves to the *teaming variety* that constitutes the inner life of men and women, children and adults.

I have emphasized that actions that flow from the core of the mind, the creative centre, expand and deepen the mind but there is an implication here that there are actions which do not originate in this creative centre. There are entities within the mind which frequently smother this inner core and many actions flow from these alien realities. The question that naturally arises is how do these become implanted in the personality? It is necessary to formulate the notion that each human being is surrounded by a protective membrane. Freud referred to this as a *stimulus barrier* and described it in *Beyond the Pleasure Principle*. He was confronted with this when soldiers in the First World War were shell shocked which meant that the explosion of a shell nearby imploded into the inner world of the soldier who was nearby and this led to a repetitive series of unplanned actions. The implosion into the inner world of foreign elements leads to actions which are not governed by any creative action from within. The way Freud envisions the *stimulus barrier* is by seeing it as if it were a heavy raincoat that kept out the rain and hail from pelting down upon the body. This protective membrane is an essential component of every organism. In particular he saw its prime role as not so much to let in stimuli but rather to keep out stimuli which were disturbing to the focus of attention. He says:

> *Protection against stimuli is an almost more important function for the living organism than reception of stimuli . . . the sense organs, which consist essentially of apparatus for the reception of certain specific effects of stimulation, but which also include special arrangements for further protection against excessive amounts of stimulation and for excluding unsuitable kinds of stimuli.*[6]

Each human being is enveloped by a membrane which allows in stimuli from the surrounding environment and also keeps out stimuli that interfere with the object which is engaging the individual's attention. Freud named this membrane the *stimulus barrier*. He emphasized, as this quote makes clear, that its capacity to prevent stimuli from entering was probably more important than its function of letting stimuli in. He also makes the point that this membrane has a differentiating function. It is able to diagnose the difference between harmful stimuli and those that are beneficial.

The term 'stimulus barrier' or 'membrane' harmonize with the model of a human being as an organism but as the thesis of this book is that the core of the personality is a creative agent, an important function of which is to keep out stimuli that it cannot process and only give entry to those that it can, so the image of a chef who selects the right ingredients to make beef stroganoff and rejects those that are unsuitable is an analogy that fits better with our conceptualization of the personality. It is the idea here that a constituent of this inner core is the capacity to choose. *Stimulus barrier* or *membrane* conjure up the image of something on the outer perimeter of the organism but what I am emphasizing here is that this function resides in the creative core of the personality. This core can choose to admit this stimulus but refuse that one.

We can however keep the term 'membrane' as long as it is clear that this is a function under the governance of the creative core. It's that the core is the creator of the membrane. So when a patient said that her membrane was too porous I take the view that the creative core has not fashioned the membrane in a mode that is beneficial for her. It has been fashioned not according to her desires, the desires of this particular person but rather according to the desires or outlook of someone else; maybe her father or her mother or an institution of which she is a member.

The functioning of the creative core depends to a large extent upon the respectful freedom given to the individual. So the mother of Stephen noticed that he tapped with a metal spoon six empty milk bottles. She then put different quantities of water in each bottle and so when her son tapped them on a subsequent occasion there was a different note emitted from each. 'He has a musical ear,' she said to herself and bought him a mouth organ and he began to play it with patience and stamina. That story ends by Stephen going to the Consortium for Music and ended by becoming the lead violinist in a national orchestra. Another son of the same mother became a first rate mathematician. This mother attended in a tuned in way to the different aspirations of her children and thus fostered the desires of their hearts. She did this by an attentive observation of each child's interests. She did not impose a subject of her own interest upon her children.

What is it that leads one person to become an historian, another a painter, another an engineer, another a musician, another an aviator, another a geologist? What inner stewardship leads one person in this direction and someone else in a different one? That there is talent that favours one particular career must be one aspect of it but there is something else. There is desire that moves **him** in one direction and **her** in another. Desire is a component part of the creative core. Desire is what gives force and impetus to the chosen vocation. But how is it that desire is of one colour in this person and of a different hue in another? Sometimes the son follows the father but sometimes son or daughter strike out in a completely different direction. Why does this one have a passion for music while this other one is dedicated to ornithology? I mentioned in the penultimate chapter the Australian aviatrix, Nancy Bird, who knew from the age of four that she wanted to be a pilot.[7] Clearly she could only have such a desire if she lived in an age and location where there were planes. If she had been born in the eighteenth century this would not have been possible. So there has to be the outer object that sends out an invitation that is accepted by this one but not the other one. But what is it that draws Michael towards being a chef and Margaret to being a travel writer? This is the conundrum for which no answer is forthcoming. It requires the recognition of *mystery*. *Mystery*, properly understood, means that the human mind is limited in its capacity to grasp that which differentiates one person from another. The aim here is to focus upon that which limits the human capacity.

We have to posit a harmony of direction between the individual and the chosen subject. Augustine of Hippo said that we become what we love. When we use the above terms: historian, painter, engineer, musician, aviator or geologist we are talking of people who are bound in their 'work-path' to a particular investigation into one aspect of the world. So when someone wants to participate in modes of being in the world, to enter and partake himself into one of these chosen fields, he then feels himself together with historians or painters or engineers. It seems that this is already in him and he wants to develop it. It means there is some knowledge of the inner aspiration. The historian or engineer is already there and known to be there. There is an appetite for this rather than that. There is some knowledge that it is not possible to be everything. So there is knowledge in the individual of his or her limitation. I have to choose one of these. 'I am a limited creature so although I should love to be an historian, a painter, an engineer, a musician, an aviator and a geologist I am forced to give myself to one of these and renounce the others.' In adolescence the individual frequently wants all at once. So, on the arrival of adulthood, there comes to me a knowledge of the wide variety of professional careers and, at the same time, a knowledge that to give of myself and become an *aficionado* in any one means making a choice. This choice seems to be dictated by aptitude and talent. If I am useless at mathematics I will probably not be drawn to becoming an engineer and if I have no talent for drawing or painting I am unlikely to become a painter but maybe I have an interest in my parents' lives and my grandparents also so then I am drawn to becoming an historian. The recognition of limitation is one of the defining aspects of adulthood.

So vistas open up of huge wide landscapes of human activity and knowledge but this is restricted in the face of this enormous pageantry of the human scene so the focus is upon what restricts the individual in his own engagement with it. It does seem that there is a kind of sympathy between this individual and one aspect of the world rather than another. Why is this person interested in birds, this one drawn to study the stars and this other one the history of the Roman Empire? We do not know but it seems that there is a something in the planetary concourse that exercises attraction upon the souls of individuals. One might call it a higher appetite, taking an analogy from taste. Foods of one kind attract this individual, foods of another attract someone different but ask one person why he likes tomatoes but not onions and he can give no rational answer. So also this same appetitive quality operates in the higher levels of psychic connection with the variety existing in the universe.

Notes

1 Chadwick, Henry (2009). *Augustine of Hippo – A Life*. p. 46. Oxford: Oxford University Press.
2 Milner, Marion (1984). *On Not Being Able to Paint*. p. 84. London: Heinemann.

3 Berenson, Bernard (1954). *The Italian Painters of the Renaissance*. p. 105. London: The Phaidon Press.
4 Tolstoy, L.N. (1869/1986). *War and Peace*. pp. 956–957. Translated by Rosemary Edmonds. Harmondsworth, Middlesex: Penguin Books.
5 Berlin, Isaiah (1979). *Against the Current*. [The Counter-Enlightenment]. p. 8. London: The Hogarth Press.
6 Freud, S. (1920). *Beyond the Pleasure Principle*. S.E.v. XVIII. pp. 27–28. London: The Hogarth Press & The Institute of Psycho-Analysis.
7 '[M]y mother mentioned that at the age of four, I was balancing on the back fence, arms outstretched, calling myself an 'eppy plane.' Bird, Nancy (1990). *My God! It's a Woman*. p. 9. Sydney: Angus and Robertson.

Chapter 9

What is it that is unconscious?

According to the schema I have been presenting in this book you might want to ask me 'Well, what is it that is unconscious?' It is a very good question because the answer is quite different from Freud's conception. For Freud something is unconscious because there is a sexual desire the knowledge of which is resisted and, because resisted, the knowledge is repressed and therefore not known. So, for instance, Freud says:

> many dreams which appear to be *indifferent* and which one would not regard as in any respect peculiar lead back on analysis to wishful impulses which are unmistakably sexual and often of an unexpected sort. Who, for instance, would have suspected the presence of a sexual wish in the following dream before it had been interpreted? The dreamer gave this account of it: *Standing back a little behind two stately palaces was a little house with closed doors. My wife led me along the piece of street up to the little house and pushed the door open; I then slipped quickly and easily into the inside of a court which rose in an incline.* Anyone, however, who has had a little experience of translating dreams will at once reflect that penetrating into narrow spaces and opening closed doors are among the commonest sexual symbols and will easily perceive in this dream a representation of an attempt at *coitus a tergo* (between the two stately buttocks of the female body). The narrow passage rising in an incline stood, of course, for the vagina.[1]

So he has the belief that what is repressed and becomes unconscious are sexual desires which are proscribed by the society in which the person lives. It is unconscious because of this social proscription. What I am going to propose is that what is unconscious is the inner creator; that what is produced is known – for instance a dream or an imaginative thought or, as was spoken of in the sixth chapter concerning the *unfocussed stare* à la Milner,[2] or *reverie* according to Bion, or which Freud called *evenly suspended attention*, or which General Smuts called a *wide roaming and exploration and surveying over large districts*[3] and which David Shulman called *the relatively unfocused, even floating, receptive attentiveness, neither inward-nor outward-directed.*[4] The creative imagery that lies behind these different formulations is what is known but what is not known is that which produces these dream-like images. I referred in the last chapter to ostensible illusions. These are illusions that have a definite shape, a distinct form. I gave examples such as I believe I am dead, I believe that I do not exist, I believe that when I die that the rest of the universe will come to an end. So the word ostensible means we are referring to a belief that has a definite form. It is ostensible; it can be described. This can be a visible image such as the sight of my mother entering my room though she died twenty years ago. It can be an audible illusion such as when I hear a voice telling me that I am hated or visible when see my Aunt Rosemary when looking at a bush. It is only later that I realize that it is the slant of the light on the bush that led me to see Aunt Rosemary. So these are visible and audible illusions but an ostensible illusion may have no visible or auditory properties but consist in a belief about the form in which my existence presents itself to me.

* * *

I want however to introduce a principle that fits better with the scheme I have been presenting. So I ask myself 'How do I determine what is the truth? How do I know whether what this person is communicating to me is the truth?' It is through a particular faculty that is able to tell us whether what is being communicated is genuine or false. What is this faculty that I am speaking of? Can you guess? Well I will tell you: it is *trust*.

I was treating a woman who was unable to pay during the initial period of time when I was treating her. I therefore told her she could pay me at an undefined date in the future when her financial circumstances had changed and the treatment sessions continued according to their natural rhythm. She commented more than once that it was a surprise to her that I had placed this trust in her. After some months she began to notice that *she* was beginning to trust people in a way that was new to her. She and I made the connection that my trust of her had predisposed her to start to trust. So this trust in her generated in her a trusting of others. I think again here is an instance of something I have emphasized. My trust of her was not just *my* trust; it was a trust that arose from the shared medium that had been created by both of us.

I want to examine the principles that underlie this. Is it trust, and trust alone, that is capable of generating a similar psychological act in the other? Or does generosity, gratitude or forgiveness have the same procreative power? I think the answer to this query is that generosity, gratitude and forgiveness may lead to an admiration, a valuing of the possessor of such virtues yet it does not, of itself, foster the same quality in him or her who sees it and reveres it though it may stimulate, from outside as it were, the desire to act similarly. But with trust it is different. When I trust someone she and I are in my inner world and her inner world. The two egos, the two creators are in a joined-up harmony. She is in me and I am in her so there arises a shared endowment. Trust means what I give you give. There is a mutual giving to each other. We are in a shared world so a giving is not one way; I give to you and you give to me. When I trust you there are two possible responses: either you alienate yourself from me; you want nothing to do with me or you join arms with me. When I trusted the lady who would pay me later when her financial circumstances were more stable I gave something to her and she gave something to me. It was this mutual inter-giving that is described as trust. But what is it that is given? It is a giving of myself into the care of the other. In this case she gave of herself and I gave of myself. Trust indicates that this is done because of a faith in the goodwill of the other.

Trust demands a response. As a mother is feeding her young child she offers to it on a spoon a bit of rice pudding. The child can either take it into its mouth or push it away. Trust is a spoonful of mental rice pudding. It can be repudiated or taken in. If it is taken in, it feeds the potency for trust within. Trust is there as a potential. It becomes actual, makes that transition from potency to act through the ingestion of a loving care in the other.

Feeding and exercise together are what constitutes a bodily state of health. Trust also has these two components. There is the taking in, the sharing and also the exercise of it subsequently. The enhancement of trust requires these two functions to happen; that first the person is trusted and then second that he or she exercises that trust. A little more needs to be said though about the 'taking in' of trust. Analogies are only ever partly right. Trust is not consumed like a piece of food from another. What is happening when I trust someone? There is some quality in the other that leads me to trust him or her. What is this quality? It is that this *other* is regarded for his or her own sake; I connect to this soul for its own sake not because I want to use him or her for some utilitarian purpose. Trust is what tells me whether someone is acting either in general or towards me in particular with a utilitarian objective and therefore I am witnessing the behaviour of someone who is an isolated alien or whether he or she is in a shared milieu with me. So is this a manifestation of two creators in a shared unity or that of an isolated alien? The latter, in outer behaviour, can look similar to the behaviour of someone together with another in shared unity but trust tells me that it does not flow from the inner creator. Trust issues from the creative core of the personality and not any subsidiary.

Before civilization was created, that great moment in our ancient history known by palaeontologists as the upper/middle Palaeolithic transition, when the sheer wonder of the world and what it was possible for humans to create came like a thunderbolt onto our planet; that prior to this startling event one human being and another joined together for the accomplishment of a task which could not be achieved by just one individual on their own; he or she needed another to be able to accomplish the task but after this supreme event two people joined for the mutual love and enjoyment of each other. So friendship was born. Cicero said that the essence of friendship is annihilated once it is subordinated to a utilitarian need. In *Laelius: On Friendship* Cicero starts this dialogue shortly after Scipio Africanus, his friend, had died so he says:

> *Consider Africanus, for example. Did he need me? Of course he did not. Nor, for that matter, did I need him. I was attached to him because I admired his fine qualities; and he returned my feelings because he also, on his side, appeared not to have formed too bad an opinion of my own character.*[5]

Trust is the foundation for the 'superior virtues' such as gratitude, generosity and forgiveness. One might ask 'Well yes, trust, but trust of what?' It is a trust that the other's prime goal when he or she encounters another is respect for that other as other rather than the use of him or her for self-enhancing advantage. Tolstoy gives in *War and Peace* an excellent example of someone whose interest in others is for his own advantage. He tells of Colonel Adolph Berg who wanted to be accepted in the higher echelons of Society. So he approached Pierre, Count Bezuhov, asking him to come to a reception at his home. Tolstoy says that Berg arrived

> *in an immaculate brand-new uniform with his hair pomaded and curled over his temples in imitation of the Emperor Alexander.*

Berg tells Pierre that he had already asked Helène, Countess Bezuhov, but that she had considered it beneath her dignity to associate with *nobodies like the Bergs*. Pierre accepts to go and then Berg says this:

> *You can always find something to imitate or ask for. Look at me now, how my life has gone since my first promotion.* [Berg measured his life not by years but by promotions.] *My comrades are still nobodies, while at the first vacancy I shall be regimental commander. . . . And how did I accomplish all this? Principally by knowing how to select my acquaintances. . . . Berg was satisfied and happy. The blissful smile never left his face. The soirée was being a great success, exactly repeating every other soirée he had been to. Everything was similar: the ladies' refined conversation, the cards, the general raising his voice over the game, the samovar and the tea cakes; only one thing was lacking, which he had always seen at the evening parties he wished to imitate. There had not yet been a loud conversation among the men and argument over some grave intellectual concern.*[6]

Tolstoy shows clearly in this chapter that Berg's interest in other people is in terms of whether they will promote his own position in society. This is primary for him and not respect for them as persons in their own right.

When we encounter malevolent people a way of describing them is to say that such a person has radically refused the gift of trust. This is what evil is. The classical definition of evil is an absence of goodness. I want to refine it here by saying that it is a total refusal of what Cicero refers to.

So when I trusted this lady, trusted that she would pay me when her financial circumstances improved, it must, I believe, have been that I sensed a quality in her of this respect for the other. I think it is that, like Cicero, the bond with the person as person is more important than any advantage that she could derive from me. It is not that she does not hope that I will give her something but that this is secondary. What is primary is her respect for me.

If this is right then when I trust someone it indicates that there is a knowledge of this particular quality – that this person values more the other for his or her own self rather than the use that can come about through knowing him or her. So trust contains a knowledge of the motivational direction of the other. It is an inherent piece of knowledge. It has to mean that there is a knowing that penetrates into the soul of the other; into his inner attitude to me; to the way he views me. There are two alternatives: that the other's connection to me is for the sake of what utilitarian advantage I can provide him or her with or that he or she values me, my company. Both these motives may be present in him or her in relation to me. The 'inferior motive' is always present but if the 'respect for the other' is obliterated entirely or almost entirely then this foments distrust in the other. Trust then is that knowledge that discriminates between these two motivational forces. It is important to realize however that no motive is ever entirely pure; there is always a mixture; what we want to know is which is dominant.

I think however it is necessary to consider that this *inherent piece of knowledge* is something learnt. At the age of about one a baby begins to walk; the baby *learns* to walk. That quote I gave from Rousseau is relevant: that when the baby recognizes its nurse it has learnt a lot. I will give you what he says again:

> *Man's education begins at birth; before he can speak or understand he is learning. Experience precedes instruction; when he recognizes his nurse he had learnt much. The knowledge of the most ignorant man would surprise us if we had followed his course from birth to the present time. If all human knowledge were divided into two parts, one common to all, the other peculiar to the learned, the latter would seem very small compared to the former.*[7]

A colleague who was treating a three-year-old boy discovered that he did not know how to swallow. When given some water to drink it spilled out of his mouth and sprayed all over the place. When still a foetus in the womb the infant does not swallow. Swallowing is something he learns to do once he is out of the womb. Yet this child had not learnt to do this. I am emphasizing the fact that all knowledge is learnt in order to underline the fact that this inherent knowledge of the motivational direction of the other is something learnt and we encounter people who have not learnt this. I have come across people who have trusted everyone. This means that the capacity to differentiate has not been learnt, that trust has not occurred. How is this kind of knowledge learnt? What needs to happen in order for it to occur? Well there is a hint in the interaction between myself and the lady whom I trusted. When I trusted her she began to trust people, some people, not everyone. In fact she also began to be able to differentiate between someone she could trust and someone she could not trust. So, for instance, she was able to see that her mother was someone unable to make decisions and therefore swung between one impulse and a contrary one. She came to realize that she could not trust her mother when she offered to help over something. So her mother said she would come once a week to help with her young four-year-old son. She came regularly for four weeks but then suddenly stopped. So Virginia was let down but although this had happened to her many times before she had still not 'realized' it. The important question is 'How did she come to realize it?' Well, in her case, it was that I had trusted her and she therefore began to trust and this enabled her to see her mother as someone who could not be trusted. Really what we are saying is that prior to this crucial event she did not have in her the capacity to trust.

An inherent element in trust is the capacity to assess the modes of functioning in the other. The first is to know whether there is in the other the basic respect, reverence almost, for another person. This is the most basic piece of knowledge contained in the term 'trust.' Then secondary to that is the assessment of a person's competencies. There is no point in trusting someone to be original if he or she lacks imagination. I listed some of these functions in Chapter 2. It would be trust misplaced if I expected someone to synthesize a variety of elements if I knew that the person in question was unable to unify; if this was a function that was poorly developed in him or her. Even the word *trust* is not quite right and I believe that trust should be maintained for that basic respect that we note in someone and that when we are talking not of this but of functions of the ego then the right word to use is judgement. Sometimes when we talk of judging someone's character we are referring to that quality which is the preserve of trust but sometimes we are talking of the assessment not of his or her moral outlook but his capability. Whether he or she is able to think, the capacity to abstract, the capacity to relate to older people, sick people or children. We make a judgement about someone's particular function. However there are some functions listed in Chapter 2 that are part and parcel of trust; for example the capacity for sympathy.

Let us provisionally put it that there are two different forces that come into play when I encounter another person. So Cicero says this:

> *Anyone who wants to allege that a friendship is formed for the sake of advantage seems to me to be doing away with the most attractive things such an association can offer. What we enjoy in a friend is not the profit we derive from him, but the affection. Any practical benefit that goes with this affection only gives satisfaction when it is the product of a warm heart.*[8]

When Cicero says that 'anyone who wants to allege that a friendship is formed for the sake of advantage' he knew that there were people who form a bond with someone for the sake of some utilitarian advantage. So that the driving bond in such a person is for the sake of his or her own advantage rather than enjoyment of the bond.

So you were expecting to hear about the Unconscious so why is Neville going on about Trust? What is it that is unconscious? At root it is not what Freud says that I quoted at the beginning. It is that we can know the productions of the creative core but we cannot know the creative core itself. I have a foot ruler at home. I want to measure the width of my desk so I take out the ruler and discover that it is three feet and six inches wide. But I cannot measure the ruler itself. I assume it is a foot long; I am stuffed with beliefs of this sort. The creative core produces dreams, reverie, free-floating attention, a wide-unfocussed gaze and these I can assess but I cannot assess the creative core itself. This is the Unconscious. And trust is the knowledge of when the outer behaviour flows from this united creative core and when it does not. The Unconscious is the creative core of the personality; Trust knows when something comes from it and when it does not. But the thing itself can never be reached. It is itself.

Notes

1 Freud, Sigmund. *The Interpretation of Dreams*. The S.E. Edition of the complete psychological works of Sigmund Freud: Vol. V, p. 397.
2 Milner, Marion (1987). *The Suppressed Madness of Sane Men*. p. 81 [The Framed Gap]. London & New York: Tavistock Publications.
3 Smuts, Jan Christiaan (1926/96). *Holism and Evolution*. p. 7. Gestalt Journal Press Inc.
4 Shulman, David (2012). *More Than Real: A History of the Imagination in South India*. p. 141. Cambridge, MA & London: Harvard University Press.
5 Cicero (1984). Laelius: On Friendship. In *Cicero on the Good Life*. p. 193. Harmondsworth, Middlesex: Penguin Books.
6 Tolstoy, L.N. (1869/1986). *War and Peace*. pp. 552–555. Translated by Rosemary Edmonds. Harmondsworth, Middlesex: Penguin Books.
7 Rousseau, Jean-Jacques (2013). *Emile*. p. 33. Mineola, NY: Dover Publications.
8 Cicero (1984). Laelius: On Friendship. In *Cicero on the Good Life*. pp. 204–205. Harmondsworth, Middlesex: Penguin Books.

Index

ability to relate 8
Absolute Being 94
Acton, Lord 51
actus intellectualis 3
Against the Current 2
aggregate delusion 58–9
aliveness: creative principle as root of 49; knowledge of 44–6; lust for coherence and 98
aloneness 35–6; versus isolation 81
alpha function 3, 4, 31, 37, 44, 49
ambition 23–4, 76–7, 104–5
Aquinas, Thomas 3, 88
Aristotle 68
art versus science and the mind 3, 84
Astonishing Hypothesis, The 60
attachment 7–8, 20
attention: concentrated quiet 101; in creative intercourse 97–8; dreamy 73–4; evenly suspended 73; forms of 72–3; free-floating 82, 107; notation and 97–8; wide roaming and exploration 74; wide-unfocussed stare 73, 75
Augustine, St. 24, 91, 96, 105
awareness 28–9; altering things 57; transmitted to the other 58

background assumptions in psycho-analytic thinking 37
beauty, making of 19
Being: Absolute 94; human life differentiated from 86; as infinite 86; knowledge of selfhood and 89–90; as object of contemplation 92–3; science and mystery of 85; tributaries flowing from knowledge of 87–8; truths in 86–7
beliefs 3–5; aggregate delusional 58–9; from God 33–6, 79–80; personal connection to 59–60; psychosis as product of 78–9; in religion 33, 78–9; struggle for survival and 15
Berenson, Bernard 63, 99
Bergson, Henri 36
Berlin, Isaiah 2, 5, 15, 102–3
beta element 31, 44
Beyond the Pleasure Principle 19, 103
bhavana 38, 40
Bion, Wilfred 11, 23, 35–7, 41; on *alpha function* 3–4, 31, 37, 44, 49; on being present in consulting 55–6; believers in 81–2; on equivalence in relationship 76; on inquiry 98; on intentions of others 57; on psycho-analysis as conversation 72, 77; on reverie 73, 77–8, 107; on state without desire or memory 23, 41, 55–6, 70
Bird, Nancy 23–4, 76–7, 104
blind paintings 25–6
Brook, Alexis 60
Burney, Christopher 89

charism 33, 79
Chesterton, G. K. 14, 84–5, 90, 91–3
Clark, Kenneth 63
Clinton, Bill 55
cognitive-behavioural therapy (CBT) 58
coherence, lust for 98, 102–3
Collingwood, R. G. 18
companionship 53
concentrated quiet attention 101
contemplation 47–8; in artistic originality 63; as goal of meditation 92–3; *see also* knowledge
Copernicus 66
core of the personality: formation and 32, 38; freedom and 16–17; functioning of

Index 115

creative centre in 23–5, 38–9; hypnotic power and 69; loss of hope and 21–2; making of beauty and 19; stimulus barrier and 19–20, 103–4; survival drive and 15–16
Cradle of Thought, The 48
creative core 19, 38–9; desire as component of 23–4, 104; functioning of 23–5; hypnotic power and 69; inner core 39–40, 86–7, 103–4; reality creation and 99–100; without *alpha function* 49
creative intercourse 96–7; attention and 97–8; concentrated quiet attention in 101
creative principle 37–8
Crick, Francis 60

Dead Man Walking, The 49–50
deep transferences 11
delusion 44, 45–6; aggregate 58–9; nature of understanding and 59; personal connection to 59–60
Descartes, René 2
desire: as component part of the creative core 23–4, 104; sexual 67; state without memory or 23, 41, 55–6, 70; vocational choice and 23–4, 76–7, 104–5
deus ex machina 90
development and deterioration, continuous 36
Different Path, A 44
distinguished people 80
dream-memory 21
dreams 31–2, 107
dreamy thoughts 73–4
drives, human 14–16
Dufy, Raoul 52
dysfunctional elements, attention on 97–8

Eckhart, Meister 67–8
ego 14, 28, 38, 56; aggregate delusion in 58–9; unformed 31
egocentrism 45
Einstein, Albert 34, 80
Enlightenment, the 2
envy 57–8
evenly suspended attention 73
evil 79
Eye and Brain 6

factual knowledge 62
Fairbairn, William E. 81
fanaticism 94

Field, Joanna 41, 69, 72
folie à deux 93
folie à millions 60, 94
forgiveness 110
formation 31–2, 37–8
formative power 4
freedom 16–17, 51–2
free-floating attention 82, 107
Freud, Anna 2
Freud, Sigmund 4, 12, 35, 58; on attention 74; believers in 81; on the ego and the id 14, 38; on evenly suspended attention 73; on forms of knowledge 88–9; on neurosis formation 73–4; on the Preconscious 56; on state without memory or desire 70; on stimulus barrier 19; on the truth 68–9; on the unconscious 107
Freudian Libido 47
friendship 109
Fromm, Erich 60, 93–4

Galileo 66
gay marriage 36, 82
generosity 108, 110
Gladwell, Malcolm 53
God: beliefs from 33–6, 79–80; imported to explain things 90–1; scientific research and beliefs about 79–80; supremacy of 64–5
Goodall, Jane 29
Gosling, Bob 90
gratitude 110
Gregory, Richard 6–7

hallucination 38–9, 58
Hardy, Thomas 49–50
Hazlitt, William 94
heliocentrism 66
Hobson, Peter 7, 8, 20, 48
Holism and Evolution 73
homosexuality, laws against 36, 82
hope, loss of 21–2
human condition 34
Hume, Basil 92
hypnotic power: artistic originality and 62–3; effectiveness of 64–5; factual knowledge and 62; individual judgment and 64; the infinite and 67–8; of love 66–7; subjectivity in relation to another and 69–70; submission to authority and 69–70

116　Index

I and the Other 45, 50
id, the 14, 38
idleness of mind 70
illusions: dream-like 107–8; ingestion of 99; lust for coherence and 98, 102–3; ostensible 11–12
imagination 5–6, 17–18; dealing with infinity 85–6; making of beauty and 19
inference 97–8
infinity 67–8, 85–6
inner creative core 39–40, 86–7, 103
inner insight/light 87–8
inner soul 73–4
inquiry 98
Institute of Psycho-Analysis 1
intangible force 101
isolation 36, 45; aloneness versus 81; psychosis as 78–9

Jaques, Elliot 43
judgment, individual 64
Jung, Carl 35, 58; believers in 81; on the truth 68

Kant, Immanuel 84, 90, 91
Keller, Helen 89
Kepler, Johannes 34, 35, 66, 80
Kingdom of God, The 62
Klein, Melanie 2, 35, 36, 74; believers in 81; on utopia 67
knowledge: of aliveness 44–6; of Being (*see* Being); factual 62; from forebears 101–2; Freud on forms of 88–9; of handicap 56–7; inherent piece of, as learnt 111; pathways to 88; transported from outside to the heart of the mind 92; *see also* contemplation
Knowledge Viewed in Relation to Learning 4
Koestler, Arthur 66
Kohut, Heinz 35, 81
Koval, Ramona 28

Laelius: On Friendship 109
language of expression 46, 53, 76, 77, 78, 101–2
learning, inherent piece of knowledge and 111
Le Milieu Divin 77
life force 101
Locke, John 2, 3, 4–5
Long Walk to Freedom 55

Lorenz, Konrad 8
love 66–7
lust for coherence 98, 102–3

Macmurray, John 4–5, 10, 44; on freedom 16
magical acts 98, 102
Mandela, Nelson 55–6
manifestation of the infinite 68
Mann, Sargy 25–8, 29
March, Peter 75
Marx, Karl 68
matter of our acquirements 4
Mayo, Elton 22, 69, 73, 75
Mcneile Dixon, W. 5–6, 34, 68, 80, 86
meditation, goal of 92–3
membrane 19–20, 103–4
memory 21; short-term 52–3; state without desire or 23, 41, 55–6, 70
Menninger Clinic 93
mental gazing 47
Milner, Marion 22, 27, 41; on hypnotic power 69; on Joanna Field 41, 69, 72; on misgivings 73; on painting 62–3; on underestimation of psycho-analytic knowledge 60; on unfocussed stare 72, 98, 107; on wide-focussed attention 75
mind, the: art versus science and 3, 84; attachment and 7–8; awareness in 28–9; beliefs and 3–5; contemplation by 47–8; Enlightenment thinking on 2–3; hallucination and 38–9; hypnotic power of (*see* hypnotic power); idleness of 70; imagination of 5–6; increased competence of 90–1; inner soul and 73–4, 103; limitations of 91, 105; memory in 21–2; and mental as synonym for relationship 75–6; ostensible illusions and 11–12; psychoanalysis and 1–2; super-ego and 9–10; wide roaming and exploration of 74–5
misgivings 73
Mitchell, David 28, 73
mothers: attachment and 7–8, 20; in connection with babies 51; primary maternal preoccupation and 48, 74
My God! It's a Woman 76
mystery 24, 91, 105

narcissism 50
narrow-focussed analytic reasoning 72–3, 98

neurosis, formation of 73–4
Newman, John Henry 3–5
Newton, Isaac 34, 80
notation and attention 97–8

On Not Being Able to Pain 62
Ontology 85, 96
ostensible illusions 11–12
Other, the 20, 28, 45; personal sharing with 37; transmitted awareness to 58
Outliers 53

pain 54–6
painting: blind 25–8; as externalization of unique rhythm of painter 27–8; Marion Milner on 62–3
Parmenides 87–8
passion and interests 15–16, 24–5
passive-aggression 46
Pasteur, Louis 15
pathways to knowledge 88
perception, division of 10
personal connection 59–60
personality, the: creator as core of 14, 17, 38; drives and 14–15; enriched by pain 55–6; Freud on 14; functions of 43–50; reality and 99–100; super-ego and 9–10; *see also* core of the personality
pleasure principle 88
poetry 22, 23, 49–50
Polanyi, Michael 47, 88
polytheism 34–5, 80
Preconscious, the 56
primary maternal preoccupation 48, 74
prisons of the spirit 5
professionalization 93
psycho-analysis 1–2; analysand or patient in 40; analyst viewed as superior in 65; background assumptions in 37; Bion on conversation of 72, 77; diversity of thought in 80–1; interpretation as agent of change in 8; in low IQ individuals 60; painting-language of 28; process in 10–11; silent patient in 41–2, 47–8, 78
psychosis 22, 32
psychosis as isolation 78–9
'Pure You' 40–1

reality, creation of 99–100
rebellion 9–10
reflection 51–2; goal of 92–3; self-confession and 55

relationships: trust in 108–13; between two objects as not physical 75–6
religion 9, 23; beliefs in 33–4, 78–9; importing God to explain things 90–1; individual judgment and 64; infinity and 67–8; scientific research and beliefs about 79–80; supremacy in 64–6
reverie 73, 77–8, 82, 101, 107
Roman Inquisition 66
Rosenthal 8
Rostov, Nikolai 64
Rousseau, Jean-Jacques 7, 37, 54, 111; on language of expression 46, 53, 76, 77, 78

secure attachment 8, 20
self-confession 55
selfhood, knowledge of 89–90
senses, the 17, 89
sexual desire 67
sexual intercourse 100
shame 45–6; envy as consequence of 57–8; as negative transference 56–7
shared experience 22
Shelley, Percy B. 18
short-term memory 52–3
Shulman, David 38, 41, 73, 74–5, 107
silent patients 41–2, 47–8, 78
Skinner, B. F. 1
Skylark, The 18
Smuts, Jan Christian 73, 74, 107
societal changes 36, 82–3
Soloviev, Vladimir 1, 16, 92
Spinoza, Baruch 91
Stilpo 40
stimulus barrier 19–20, 103–4
submission to authority 69–70
suffering of pain 54–6
Sullivan, Mary Ann 89
super-ego 9–10; presence of harsh 44, 45
supremacy 64–6
survival, struggle for 15–16
Suttie, Ian 47

tabula rasa 2, 3
tacit knowledge 47, 52
'taking in' 52
Tavistock Clinic 60, 90, 92, 93
teaming variety 103
Teilhard de Chardin, Pierre 77
theory of knowledge 1
theory of personal morality 1

Thompson, Francis 23
Tillich, Paul 86, 93
Tolstoy, Leo 36, 62, 64, 66, 70, 100–1, 110
Toynbee, Arnold 14, 22–3
transference 11
traumatic experiences 20–1
trust 8–9, 88, 108–13
truth 68–9, 86; teaming variety and 103; trust and 108–13
two-ness 9
Two Principles of Mental Functioning 88

unconscious, the 12; defining 107; trust and 112–13
understanding, nature of 59
unfocussed gaze *see* reverie
unfocussed stare 72, 82, 107; narrow 72–3, 98; wide 73–6; wide roaming and exploration 74, 82

Unfocussed Stare, The 72
unformed ego 31
utopia 67

Vico, Giambattista 1, 2–3
vision, sense of 17–18, 89
vocational path 23–4, 76–7, 104–5

War and Peace 64, 100–1, 110
White, Gilbert 31
wide roaming and exploration 74, 82, 107
wide-unfocussed stare 73, 75; and relationship between two objects as not physical 75–6
Winnicott, Donald 36, 48, 74, 82
Wittenberg, Isca 92
Wittgenstein, Ludwig 9, 55
work-path 23–4, 76–7, 104–5